STUDENT SUCCESS

Managing Your Future
through
Success at University and Beyond

by
Terry D. Anderson, PhD
Professor
University of the Fraser Valley, Abbotsford, BC

Sia Samimi, MA
Chair and Faculty
Northern Alberta Institute of Technology, Edmonton, AB

Kelly Bohl, BA
Master's Degree Student
Simon Fraser University, Burnaby, BC

Order this book online at www.trafford.com
or email orders@trafford.com

Most Trafford titles are also available at major online book retailers.

Printed in Victoria, BC, Canada.

ISBN: 978-1-4269-3093-5 (sc)
ISBN: 978-1-4269-3094-2 (e)

Our mission is to efficiently provide the world's finest, most comprehensive book publishing service, enabling every author to experience success. To find out how to publish your book, your way, and have it available worldwide, visit us online at www.trafford.com

Trafford rev. 4/15/2010

www.trafford.com

North America & international
toll-free: 1 888 232 4444 (USA & Canada)
phone: 250 383 6864 • fax: 812 355 4082

STUDENT SUCCESS

Managing Your Future

through

Success at University and Beyond

Table of Contents

Preface

The Overarching Purpose of this Book

Whether you are a student, teacher, administrator, or parent, the realization of your potential in and after school is a shared objective. Yet, the road to academic success remains as unpaved and choppy as ever for some. That is precisely why we decided to write this book. We wanted to go beyond the motivational speeches teachers and parents resort to in an effort to improve the student's academic results. We wanted to get to the substance of academic success, get to the practical stuff, and share behaviours and skills that helped thousands of our students meet academic and future objectives - not their parents', but their own.

We, too, have delivered motivational speeches numerous times to our students or children, often inconsequentially. For variety, we even mix it up and change the words here and there, but the main sound track usually plays the same tune. The speech begins with a sentence that has a "you must" or “you can't” somewhere in it. Some students know the oration by heart. They know the jig is up as soon as we mumble the first few words. Like a screenplay memorized and practiced to perfection, the actors involved in this often-times dramatic presentation play their part verbatim. As we dole out large dosages of advice, the listener's response to our precious offering is automatic and often predictable: Arms get crossed, eyes roll, and a wide, long invisible wall goes up. We subsequently take the futile, inevitable plunge into what seemed like an empty pool. What ensues is an irritating sigh of displeasure from the parental advice giver: "You just don't care".

But is it so? Don't our children or students care? For parents and teachers, shifting the blame to students seems logical! Yet, assuming a defensive posture by all involved almost always misses the opportunity to dig deeper for meaning and causes. Worse yet, we fail to notice what the student is NOT saying.

What Students are Really Saying: Give us Tools and Knowledge!

The truth is: Our current batch of students - often called Generation Y - are different. They think differently, they behave differently (like we didn't when we were young!), and they have very different definitions for life, prosperity, and success. Countless books have been written about Gen Ys. Numerous researchers have tried to better understand the needs, expectations and tendencies of the young generation.

What is emerging gradually is that in order for us teachers to help our students succeed, we need to not only be sympathetic, but also empathetic. We need to put ourselves “in their shoes” to realize what they “really” need and how we can help them to it. The moment we do that, we behold - standing right before us in our classes - a very different kind of student than we had assumed.

What if our students actually care a lot about life, goals, and learning? What if they just need effective tools to mange them all, tools devised by caring individuals who can look beyond cookie-cutter, age-old adult education philosophies and who are willing to help the leaner devise a personalized, customized, and deeply motivating plan of learning? But this is a road less traveled by most educators, because it requires that most precious universal commodity: time. It takes energy to assess individual needs and develop personal strategies for success when there are tens and hundreds of students in a class. A teacher might perish under the heavy load, some of us educator might say! However, while our educational systems may not be up to the task, we, the faculty, can be. To do so, we must first narrow the gap between ourselves and our students, replacing motivational speeches with practical advice that speaks to the core beliefs and needs of the students themselves. Sounds hard? Well, it is not. We just need to open up our minds to new "possibilities", a word dear to any self-respecting member of Gen Y, like you!

It is Up to You: You Create Your Own Success with the Tools We Provide

The truth is that years after you have graduated, no one will remember how often you met your instructor for help or asked questions in class. It will not matter. Many of us who call ourselves teachers (professors, lecturers, instructors, etc....) will go the extra mile to help you, if we were only approached and if you showed that you truly cared and were willing to assume part of the responsibility for your learning.

When we hear genuine concerns in our offices, when students do not shift blame and instead look for constructive solutions, we get energized and will do our utmost to pave their learning. This is nothing but the truth! It is the same in any other situation. When we blame others for something missing in our lives, usually we don't get what we want. When, on the other hand, we approach the resolution of problems as a shared responsibility and avoid blame, others will do their utmost to help us. The same with teachers. We would sacrifice lesson preparation, marking, research, administrative work, and our private lives to connect with and guide you. Using "emotional intelligence" - a critical topic we will pick up in a bit - pays huge dividends in school.

We don't want to sound like angels! Truthfully, we benefit equally from solid relationships with our students. If we can instil in your hearts and minds the desire for life-long learning, we are elated. We are exhilarated when we watch our students learn. For some of us, it is a form of intoxication! For most teachers, there is no joy more satisfying than watching their students graduate with pride, confidence, and a sense of purpose. After all, we have embraced learning as a way of life too. Much of that life involves you. Your success validates what we do and inspires us to excel in doing it.

Our Central Concern: Your Success

We three authors have, if you combine our experience, been students for over 50 years, and have taught for over 40 years in colleges or universities. We have seen countless students where success in school and beyond has unnecessarily eluded them, resulting in vast numbers never reaching their full academic or career potential... and then going off to work in jobs they hate. This book is for both students who have had frustrating experiences with school and want to see a way through, and for those who have had great success and want even more.

To some students, having a stimulating and thriving learning experience appears as imposing an obstacle as the Great Wall of China - seemingly impenetrable. Instead of excitement about learning and its limitless professional possibilities, they often anticipate the doom of failure or mediocrity hovering overhead in much of their academic pursuits. With these students' futures hanging in the balance, prospects for a fulfilling life give way to silent feelings of inadequacy and self-defeat. Their learning is further compromised by misunderstandings about their academic under-performance and misplaced comments and advice offered by people who don't understand their frustrations. In this book we will address such feelings of inadequacy. To some degree, we have all likely experienced this kind of frustration. We see students feeling this way even when they are "A" students, yet fear that they might not be admitted to law school because of the stiff competition.

As struggling students begin to develop a distorted view of themselves, believing that they are just not smart enough, good enough, or talented enough, their confidence in reaching their academic and career goals gradually erodes, resulting in even poorer results. They frequently stop seeking or using the multitude of resources available to them: partnering with peers, asking questions in class, taking advantage of tutorial opportunities, and probing their teachers for help. This agonizing, heart-wrenching cycle continues until either the students give up, drop out, or accept it as the normal state of affairs.

For us faculty, the unfolding of this drama time and time again is perhaps one of the most difficult parts of our work. For parents, too, tackling the needs of an under-achiever presents perplexing challenges. We want the best for our students, yet often feel helpless, unable to reach out or address the core issues plaguing what could otherwise be exciting years of learning and discovery.

So, what is the problem? What is the root cause of the learning deficit or block some students seem to experience? Is it us, the faculty? Perhaps our teaching is so archaic that it no longer caters to the true needs of the current generation. Is it the parents? Perhaps they have forgotten that they also faced challenges - albeit different ones - in school. Our society, possibly? Does it not distract us from what matters? Does it not place exceeding importance on immediate gratification and the pursuit of personal pleasures? Then there is the Internet, often cited as the prime instigator when investigating impediments to learning. While cyberspace can be an immeasurably resourceful instrument for learning, it can also become an alienating or addictive world, devoid of resemblance to reality. Many of our students fall prey to its trappings, drowning themselves in an isolating sea of games, chat, downloads and clicks, unable to concentrate on goals central to their long-term development personally, academically, and professionally.

But we have missed the main actor in this drama: the student. When faced with poor or unsatisfactory academic performance, it may be natural to blame learners. After all, we may reason, they should know better; they are adults and should know how to act, plan, and use their internal resources for a prosperous future. Right? Perhaps. It sure sounds reasonable.

Conversations about students and their learning habits are common among faculty in colleges and universities. While there is the occasional sharing of success stories, despondent views such as "our students are no longer the same calibre as they used to be" are frequently heard in dialogues among faculty. Often, teachers cite articles they have read or their own direct experience to vehemently support the viewpoint that today's students lack motivation and desire to succeed. Yet, the credibility of these assertions is hardly ever established. There is some support for the claim that we, the faculty, are indeed faced with a new kind of student. Some authors have suggested that student demands, expectations, abilities, and aspirations are different now as compared to the past. Yet, others, including the authors of this book, maintain that today's students have the same learning potential as the generations past, with one main difference: they learn differently and have different learning needs.

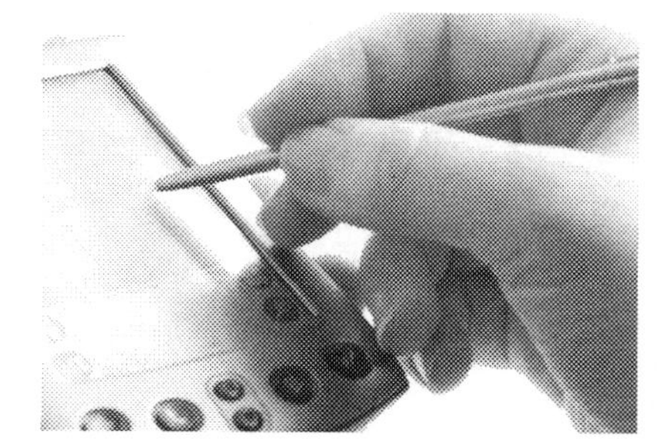

To test this hunch, look no further than the hallways in academic institutions. You will find many more mobility-enabled iPhones, laptops, and smart phones than books. Students now use digital technologies for entertainment, to get informed and to interconnect, seamlessly. They not only get much of the information they need on-line, they rely on it as the source of answers. Facebook is now used as a verb! While the lure of the on-line experience can be certainly addictive, there are no longitudinal studies found that suggest that the student today is inherently different in their ability to grasp, retain, and apply new knowledge. Neither can the cynics substantiate the inference that the Internet by itself is the cause of poor performance in post secondary education.

While our tendency may be to blame or absolve ourselves of the responsibility to deal with the real issues at play, teachers and parents must look beyond our presumptions. Our prime responsibility as teachers is to inspire our students. If they are not motivated to engage in effective learning, does that mean they are lazy? If they are not excited by the content we teach and the methodologies we employ, does that imply their indifference toward success? If they perform poorly in their courses, does that signify that they are not up for the task intellectually?

Before we can even raise the topic of academic performance and ways to enhance it, we must first examine the foundational force behind all human endeavours: **motivation**. Numerous ideas have been proposed in books, articles, and scientific journals about enhancing learning in school. There is a plethora of advice available, covering a range of topics from self-assessment to career counselling to improving memory recall and studying techniques. Student success courses attempt to prepare the student for the rigors and demands of an academic life. But what is the efficacy of such measures? Our lectures on student success may be just that: - lectures. We need to use a voice that resonates with our students, one that they can relate and connect to.

An Open Book to Students

This book is primarily intended for you, the student. These introductory remarks may not seem as though they are directed to you, but they just seem that way! As you will soon see, you were at the centre of the inception, development, and culmination of all the ideas that made up this book. In fact, students helped develop this book by providing feedback and suggesting revisions to it for several years. Even the main topics of this book were driven by students who told us what they needed and wanted in a book like this.

This Book

We set out to investigate what seems like a continental divide separating some students and their teachers. We became convinced that there was need for a no-nonsense, evidence-based set of strategies to encourage our student to see - for themselves and not for others - their own potential for success and ways to remove obstacles in their learning. Without veering into philosophical discourses on the prefect class, the perfect teacher, and the perfect student, we wanted to contribute - in our own small way - to the object of any teacher's desire: to see more of our students succeed.

In a way, writing this book started when our respective careers in post-secondary system began years ago. We subconsciously penned these pages as we taught thousands of students, heard their grievances, attempted to allay their fears about learning, and experimented with all the teaching techniques we knew, some that worked and some that did not. We wrote these paragraphs as we struggled to better understand and appreciate our students' true needs, and not our perceptions of them. The more frankly and openly we spoke with them, the more inspired we became to publish this book. We had noticed that some of our students - the ones marginalized by the one-size-fits-all educational system - felt isolated and alone. The pressures on our students mount from all directions. Peers demand a social life; teachers expect commitment to learning; and parents want a perfect child, one who spends less time on trivial pursuits and more on goals, career success and a fulfilling life.

There is little doubt that everyone involved in a student's learning journey means well. However, our efforts should be well-placed. Mere advice does not necessarily inspire a young adult to action. Effective counsel offers more than wisdom; it must be relevant to the recipient's mindset, needs, and goals. Consequently, we believe effectual learning is applied, practical, and highly personal.

Speaking of "practical," that's exactly what this book offers. Our ultimate goal is to enhance your learning, improve results, and, hopefully, make learning fun.

Chapter one investigates some of the challenges students face today, including the expectations of the 21st Century from adults - student or otherwise - and what these expectations mean with respect to a successful career.

Chapter two discusses how our brain absorbs and retains information. It will also offer some effective techniques for memory recall and preparation for exams.

Great research and skilful writing are two of the challenges students often face in school. **Chapter three** will address these topics and present techniques for effective writing, as well as using technology to create powerful presentations.

Chapter four treats learning as a profession. To do well in your job, you need to know your job description, how it will be assessed, and how good performance leads to future advancement.

In **Chapter five**, we will de-mystify learning styles. We will delve into the whole notion of intelligence and how it is (practically) defined and how it (truly) applies to you and your long-term objectives.

Chapter six builds a strong financial case for being successful academically. It speaks to the obstacles students face in school and how you can effectively take ownership, and leadership, of your learning.

Chapter seven takes a look at long-term goals. It will highlight key attributes of a purposeful life in school and how to set meaningful, personal, and achievable goals.

Learning is not dissimilar to sports. You have a game, a goal, and a strategy. **Chapter eight** will explore how you can use your natural abilities and existing talents to strategize to win the learning game.

So what **do** students want from instructors and professors? We wanted to know too, so **Appendix A** provides some insights that may help you as students just as it may help us as teachers.

Stress management is a must if you want to succeed in school. **Appendix B** outlines how you can manage and alleviate some of the common pressures in academic life.

ACKNOWLEDGEMENTS

We would like to recognize Dr. Darryl Plecas for starting the idea for this book and encouraging us to continue to develop it. We also thank three classes of our students who gave us feedback about the first pilot version of this book.

Introduction

**Designing your own life is possible to some degree.
The more you believe it is, the more it is!**

The foundation of this book is an irrefutable fact: Academic success offers great return on investment. The strong relationship between excelling academically and succeeding professionally is a reality. The higher and more successfully you climb the academic ladder, the higher your gains professionally and, ultimately, personally. Of course this does not mean that academic success is the only gateway to a successful life. Look no further than Bill Gates, a school drop out, for proof. But it is safe to say that in general doing well in school is imperative if you are aiming for a rewarding life. Decisions you make today, and the extent to which you are willing to delay gratification to meet higher objectives, will have a direct bearing on your future. Your daily choices - social life, entertainment, hobbies, and studies - greatly impact the kind of life you will enjoy and the level of satisfaction you will derive from your careers and personal endeavours.

Studying is not easy for most. In the often bewildering maze of assignments, exams, and school life, it is hard to connect day to day life (getting out of bed, heading to classes, meeting deadlines) to future prospects. Some nagging questions interrupt your daily academic routine: Why do I have to do this? What is the point of this class? How does this stuff relate to my life and goals?

Let's be honest. Most of you don't see a need to learn how to be successful at college and university. We know! You approach the whole educational experience, sight unseen, as if having a readiness to learn was a non-issue. And this, we can tell you, is where most students make their first JUMBO mistake. In fact, one aim of this book is to keep you "turned on" to college, keep you studying, and set you up for a realistic, positive learning experience. No need to settle for less than what you had hoped for, either. Academic success in not only possible, it is attainable.

We don't know exactly why students don't understand that they need to learn how to be successful at university. Could it be because your performance was average or better at high school, and you look at college as being much the same, except that you have to work a little harder? Another JUMBO mistake (number 2, but who's counting!) Truthfully, high school life ends right after the last dance at your graduation prom. At that very moment, you begin walking across a bridge that takes you to adulthood, university life, careers, family, children and a life of decisions, compromises, victories and setbacks. The reality is that when you enter university life, most of you are not prepared for the new life style and skills it takes to succeed. You seem to need an "incubation period," where you can gradually get accustomed to a very different set of values and expectations. Sure, you roll with the punches, hoping that "somehow it will all turn out." But, it does not always.

It is very easy to be intimidated by that first year in school, misunderstand the point of it all, feel over-burdened, and get so far behind. Gradually, you feel that you just can't do it all. In the end, it is easy to get discouraged, disappointed with yourself, and just plain turned off by the whole experience. Don't take our word for it. Try finding a single student who has been through their first year who will tell you otherwise. You won't find many. Then talk to the people who end up dropping out within their first year. There are plenty of them around.

We don't want to belabour the point, but we do want you to appreciate what your initial experience at college or university can do to the life path you set for yourself. We have seen how predictably most students will react when their first year doesn't go as well as they expected. What they do, in effect, is go through a rationalization process where they lower their aspirations. They start coming up with new life goals for themselves that fit these lower aspirations. They quit thinking in terms of what kind of life they **want** and start thinking in terms of what kind of life they should **settle for**. Students get sucked right into it, and that's sad because it's so preventable.

Your success inherently has multiple facets. There is no one suggestion or idea that could or would propel each and every one of you to success. However, what we have found - and this is good news - is that doing well in school is not all that complex. We humans are infinitely unique and have attributes that set us apart. But, we also have much in common. When it comes to effective learning, most of us are inspired or discouraged in similar ways. If school does not meet our needs, we lose interest. If we are not clear about the application and purpose of what we are learning, we are not eager to develop new skills. If we do not get the help we need, we drop out. Our attempt in this book, then, is to zero in on the common attributes that enhance your learning, speak to your needs, and remove obstacles you will encounter in your academic life.

How, you might ask? We will help you to be aware and clear about two things: what you are getting yourself into, and what's expected of you. To that end, we first ask you to consider your initial college or university experience as a job you have been hired to do. Additionally, we ask you to be mindful of the "success blockers" that typically interfere with a student's capacity to do the job well. This is one way to approach the experience that our own students report being helpful, though it certainly is not the only way.

We want you to do well. Accordingly, most of this book will focus on strategies you can employ to be successful in university. For instance, we will give you tips on how to:

- Organize your time
- Improve your memory
- Read faster and more effectively

- Get the most out of lectures and textbooks
- Prepare for exams
- Write essays

To do well, you don't need to carry out all of the tips we offer, but we are confident about this much: everyone reading this book (or other books like it) will find the learning process easier and more enjoyable than students normally do, even if all you do is adopt a few of our main suggestions. They will also help you to achieve better grades than you otherwise would.

Managing Your Future

Many of the skills needed for success in university or college are also those needed for success in life in the 21st century. In this book we have identified easily-learned skill-sets and have compressed them into a self-assessment and development program. As you read each chapter of this book, you can immediately rate and implement your success skills.

These same skills, once developed, can grow into strong abilities, and will help you to manage your future life and careers successfully. You will identify and remove obstacles to success, and move ahead with a clear personal vision toward an extraordinary future.

Why learn to succeed? Technology and computers are revolutionizing how we do everything. Computers are becoming so sophisticated that it is getting more and more difficult to get to the top of the field of computer science. As the field grows, only the most advanced minds will make meaningful contributions. This will be true in many occupations.

As well, the information explosion we see now will continue to accelerate, demanding higher levels of expertise and specialization. We will all have to become exceptional information managers throughout our lives, realizing that whatever information we find today may be outdated or updated tomorrow. The environment is changing, becoming more like an advanced level XBox® game rather than the predictable place it once resembled. We will have to develop a new level and ability to manage this change, which can open the way to our success. This book offers you an opportunity to learn some of the critical skills to manage change that you will need to succeed at college or university and beyond.

Changes You Will Face

In this millennium, huge changes will continue coming at us at lightning speed. For example:

- Unprecedented global opportunities for learning and international trade will present themselves.
- The whole world will be so accessible through technology and travel that it will figuratively be shrunk to only a fraction of its present size.
- Communication will be ever faster and more efficient.
- Social networking tools - such as Facebook and MySpace - will dramatically change the way knowledge is shared and passed on, easily transcending geographical boundaries.

But not all change will be for the better:

- The gap between the rich and the poor will increase. There will be less for more people.
- Governments will become less capable of caring for expanding populations of people.
- Crime, national and international crises, and strife between people and groups of people will likely increase as a result of society becoming more fragmented politically, economically and ideologically.
- The health of our environment will continue to be seriously threatened.

With these global changes blowing in the wind, you will also have to make some personal adjustments. More specifically, you will have to learn to face the following changes effectively:

- Be capable of dealing with high technology and high "touch" (quality communication and service) in most jobs.
- Learn to constantly improve and hone your skills.
- Develop all seven of your intelligences (we will discuss this later in this book), not just one or two. Act as a person with "mind power" and not just personal power.
- Follow personal and human priorities, respecting others on your work team, not "just following" institutional rules.

- Enjoy a lifetime of careers, not one lifetime career.
- Benefit from increasingly multi-cultural, multiracial and dual gender learning and working environments.
- Work in self-managed teams as a team member rather than on your own or under the direction of one person.
- Adapt to the economic and family changes associated with an aging population.
- Discover the importance of your spiritual journey so that you can make some kind of sense of your world.

Success Strategies for Managing the Changes You Will Face in this New Millennium

In the wake of these challenging trends, this book will assist you to do the following:

- Learn how to specifically detail an ennobling vision for your future.
- Discover more definition in your sense of purpose for your life.
- Clarify your identity (including your own "voice", your style, strengths, talents and interests).
- Set motivating goals to stimulate your achievement.
- Identify blocks to success and set out plans to remove them.

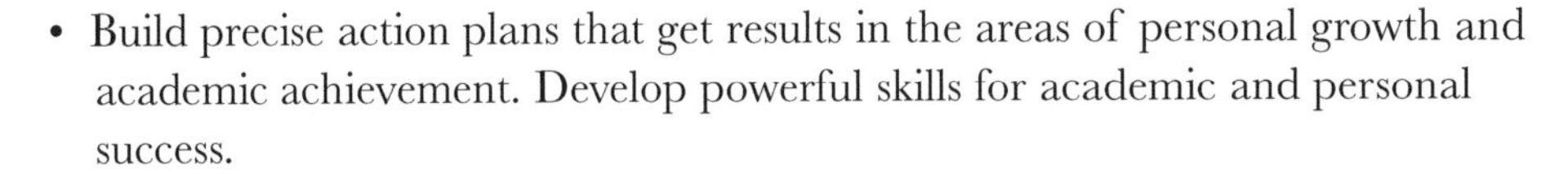

- Build precise action plans that get results in the areas of personal growth and academic achievement. Develop powerful skills for academic and personal success.
- Learn career preparation skills, professional attitudes and self-presentation skills which will help you to compete in the job market and to develop credibility in order to gain promotions throughout your career(s).
- Clarify your beliefs, purpose, values and goals, which will give you greater clarity of vision in approaching the future.

Why You Need This Book

Students in our Student Success courses have expressed the needs outlined below as those which were most critical to their personal and academic success. To get the most benefit from this book, please indicate the extent to which you think you have the following needs:

5	4	3	2	1
I Very Strongly Need to Develop in This Area	I Strongly Need to Develop in This Area	Need to Develop in This Area	Slightly Need to Develop in This Area	I Don't Need to Develop In This Area at All

Insert a number from 1 to 5 in each of the 15 spaces provided below. When you have finished reviewing these 15 common needs, you can add your total score and determine the extent to which you think your needs match what will be presented in this book.

15 Success Needs of Students

The following needs have been identified by hundreds of students as being critical to their success at school and beyond.

_____ **I Need to Understand the Demands of My Job of Student.** You may not think of being a student as a full- or part-time job which will result in payment. But it is, paid in future earnings. As a student, you have a very unique and complex job to do. Chapter 4 reveals your job description as a student, and your strengths and weaknesses in relation to the job. You will be able to gear up for success when you know what you need to do.

_____ **I Need a Motivating Personal Identity a World View, and Goals To Build On.** When you begin to understand who you believe you are, why you believe it is important for you to move ahead successfully, and what your talents, strengths, interests, assumptions, values, goals and career plans are, you will be building your foundation for motivation and success. You will develop a well-defined world view (set of beliefs and assumptions) about what is going on here, and what it all means. You will also develop a sense of purpose, and realistic but challenging goals for the future. Chapter 4 examines this important part of your success - clarity about you!

_____ **I Need to Create and Manage My Personal and Professional Image.** Your personal image, once clarified, can show up in all the academic work you do, the way you dress, talk, and walk. Image management is an important skill which you can learn to create credibility in the minds of your instructors, interviewers, employers and acquaintances. It involves the presentation of your strengths and talents in a way that fits the needs of those you wish to serve. This skill, outlined in Chapter 8, will enhance your success in all areas of life.

_____ **I Need to Learn How to Manage Information.** Knowledge is now the exchange for value, not cash or goods. You will always need knowledge skills to research and use important information to solve complex problems and create new solutions fast. Understand how to become a "lean, mean information machine" for your future. The skills of researching, organizing, memorizing and communicating information can be developed. Chapter 2 shows you some tested methods, preferred by students, to enhance your success in this area.

_____ **I Need to Set Quality-Conscious Goals.** You want higher grade point averages to win in the job market. You will learn how to achieve your best performance possible to compete in a world which is obsessed with excellent performances. You will learn to continuously improve your own performance standards and predict how well you will likely perform in each course. Chapter 7 helps you to learn how to set your own goals and standards, and increase the effectiveness of your performance as a student.

_____ **I Need to Discover and Remove Blocks to My Success.** Do you practice any self-defeating behaviours which may get in the way of success? For example, poor time management, procrastination, low standards of quality, addictions to TV, food, alcohol, drugs, or perhaps another block? Chapter 4 will assist you to identify them, develop a plan for their control or removal, and get on with your success.

_____ **I Need to Learn How to Get My Life in Order to Set the Stage for Success.** Is your study area set up? Your finances arranged? Are you committed to being a student? There is a formula for success in academics and in life and it includes being organized, having a place to work quietly for concentrated periods of time, and having a base of financial stability. Chapter 7 will assist you to set your priorities, and launch you to success.

_____ **I Need to Learn to Know Myself as a Learner.** Understand your Personal Style, and develop your Seven Intelligences. Though only two or three of your seven Intelligences are required for success at school, all of them are required for career and life successes. These include Linguistic Intelligence,

Musical Intelligence, Logical Mathematical Intelligence, Spatial Intelligence, Bodily Kinesthetic Intelligence, Interpersonal Intelligence and Intrapersonal Intelligence. You will learn about your Seven Intelligences in Chapter 5, and about your personal style and its impact on how you learn.

_____ **I Need to Learn to Get the Meat Out of a Lecture.** You need laser focus to extract the points from a lecture that will ensure success on exams and papers. Unfortunately, many lecturers may not seem stimulating or interesting to you, although lectures are the typical means of transmitting information. In Chapter 2 you will learn methods to get the most from a lecture and make each lecture count for you.

_____ **I Need to Learn to Target for Exam Items. *Get Ready!*** Exams are here to stay. Are you ready? Target for exams, identify items mentioned in lectures that will likely show up on a test, and ensure that the items you have targeted are as complete as possible. In Chapter 2 you will learn to be as prepared as possible for each exam.

_____ **I Need to Learn General Skills to Prepare for and Take Tests.** Whether it's testing for college or university entrance, testing in class, or testing for job knowledge, skills, mental abilities and personality/job fit, tests are here to stay. Chapter 2 tells you how to get ready to deal with test anxiety, overcome fear of failure, and improve your test scores on multiple choice and essay exams.

_____ **I Need to Learn a System to Rehearse Targeted Items. *Aim!*** You have identified what items will likely be on an exam. Now you will learn to rehearse correct answers to exam questions until you know that you know. This critical, but often omitted, step outlined in Chapter 2 lowers test anxiety, increases test scores and increases confidence for future tests.

_____ **I Need to Learn Techniques to Increase Test Scores. *Fire!*** You have rehearsed each exam item until you know it. But there are some things you can do while you are completing the test that will result in better scores on both multiple choice and essay exams. These techniques, outlined in Chapter 2, can increase your overall test scores from 5-10% points or more on each exam.

_____ **I Need to Learn to Research, Structure, Write and Edit Papers.** Approximately 40% - 60% of your final grade will depend upon how well you can research, structure, write and edit your papers. You can improve your grades if you master this critical survival and success skills of the writing process. The steps and techniques involved in writing a quality paper at the college or university level are often not learned in high school, but Chapter 3 primes you for success in writing papers.

_____ **I Need to Learn to Manage Stress, Time and Energy.** Deal with stress, time pressures, and low energy. With the increasing pressures of school and future planning, you may feel out of control. Chapter 9 will help you understand the basics you will need to know about stress in order to deal with the time-pressured lifestyle of being a part time or full time student.

How to Interpret Your Score

60 - 70	I strongly need to develop in the 15 success areas.
50 - 59	I need to develop in many of the 15 success areas.
40 - 49	I have moderate concerns in the 15 success areas.
30 - 39	I have slight concerns in many of the 15 success areas.
20 - 29	I am relatively unconcerned about the 15 success areas.

As you consider your needs revealed in the above survey, you may want to review the 15 need areas and prioritize them in order of their importance to you. You can do this by placing a number beside each of the 15 needs listed below. These needs are the motivating forces for you to move ahead toward success. You can also add needs that you feel should belong on the list and rank them where you want in your priority list.

Success Tip

Rank the success learning needs (page below) in order of priority and post it below where you can see it on your desk or mirror. If you look at it often, you will be reminded of why you think this course is important to you, and what you need to learn to become more successful.

Post Priority List

_____ I Need to Understand the Demands of My Job of Student

_____ I Need a Motivating Personal Identity and World View, and Goals To Build On

_____ I Need to Create and Manage My Personal and Professional Image

_____ I Need to Learn How to Manage Information

_____ I Need to Set Quality-Conscious Goals

_____ I Need to Discover and Remove Blocks to My Success

_____ I Need to Learn how to Get My Life in Order to Set the Stage for Success

_____ I Need to Learn to Know Myself as a Learner

_____ I Need to Learn to Get the Meat Out of a Lecture

_____ I Need to Learn to Target for Exam Items: Get Ready!

_____ I Need to Learn a System to Rehearse Targeted Items: Aim!

_____ I Need to Learn Techniques to Increase Test Scores: Fire!

_____ I Need to Learn to Research, Structure, Write and Edit Papers

_____ I Need to Learn to Manage Stress, Time and Energy

_____ Other: ______________________________

_____ Other: ______________________________

Chapter Two

Become a Lean, Mean Information Machine

Learning is not compulsory... neither is survival.
W. EDWARDS DEMING

How Well You Handle Information Determines Your Success

Most people have not pushed their brains even close to the limits of their capacity to process information, recall it, and do something creative with it. This has been especially true since the advent of television. The primary reason for this is that most people don't need to until they go to college. The second reason is that most people don't know how to push the limits of their performance when it comes to managing information.

What most jobs will require in the future is a certain amount of intelligent information handling. We are entering an information age in which the way we handle knowledge and information can make the difference between being wise or not. Wisdom can be considered as our effectiveness in handling information and knowledge. How we deal with information, solve problems, report information and predict the future using current information will determine, to some extent, our individual and collective destinies. Information without wisdom is foolish and sometimes even dangerous! For example, think about what could be done with the knowledge of how to split an atom if the information and technology were in destructive hands. It is with this in mind that we look toward a more inclusive and practical definition of learning.

Adopting a Practical and Motivating Definition of Learning

How you define learning will sometimes control how you approach it. If you define learning in the somewhat typical "garbage in, garbage out" manner that is used to describe much of the meaningless memorization that goes on in education, you will feel negatively about learning. If you look at learning as a rehearsal for your next real life performance, then it suddenly becomes very relevant. Try on this definition of learning and see how you like it.

> **Learning:** the internalization of the ability to respond more effectively and appropriately for the common good.

If you define learning in this way, you will see that every academic task can be used to strengthen your knowledge base, your ability to handle information, and your chances of being perceived as a professional and of making a valuable contribution. If you are well read, and can write and speak fluently, you will be recognized for this. If you decide you want to become a person who can respond to your future job more effectively and appropriately (so you are above average and get promoted), you can do so by adopting this functional perspective on learning. If you view learning as a necessary evil, consisting of a bunch of stuff that must be memorized, then your motivation, performance and morale will be on the decline.

Understanding How Your Brain Processes Information

Processing Information for Retrieval

We have asked students in many student success courses, "How many times do you read a chapter and review your notes prior to taking a multiple choice exam?" The average student answer was 2.5 times.

What do a number of studies indicate about the number of repetitions the average person has to expose their brain to in order to recall one piece of simple information with 85% or better accuracy? The average answer was seven times. Or, for more complex information, rehearse until you can demonstrate over 85% recall on demand.

This amount of repetition is what is required just for accurate recall of information. But this doesn't say anything about a person's ability to wisely do something with the knowledge they have just recalled. The creative and appropriate application of knowledge is measured by your ability to put ideas onto paper in written assignments, projects and essay exams. We will get to strategies for creative applications later in this chapter. For now we will focus on the management of information that must be recalled accurately, such as on multiple-choice, true-false and short answer exams.

It's no wonder many students worry about exams, have anxiety attacks, sweaty palms and sleepless nights before (and during) exams! They have not tested themselves enough times to prove to themselves that they know the material. They expect themselves to be able to read the text book, read over the notes they took in class, and then recall information at a better than 60% recall rate (the minimum required for passing most exams). Less than half of students succeed using their typical approach if we look at the drop out rate in the first year of college (40%-50% of students aren't there for their second year at many colleges and universities).

But I Don't Have Time to Read the Book Seven Times!

Of course you don't. We didn't either. We had jobs throughout our university careers. We had families during our Ph.D. programs. We had to come up with a system of studying that would enable us to become very efficient at organizing, processing, internalizing and retrieving information on tests. Each of us came up with our own systems that worked. The one we have tested with hundreds of students is the one we are going to share with you. It is the system that they tell us that they prefer.

The Secret Method and the Game of *"Incredible Recall"*

There are essentially three stages to the secret method in its simplest form: READY, AIM, FIRE! This "secret" method is as old as the hills and twice as dusty. Think of the game *Incredible Recall* as being similar to the game of darts, and similar to the sports of crossbow, archery or rifle shooting. In order to get good at these games or sports, you must practice over and over and over again until your skill improves. Similarly, to master information recall, you will need repeat exposures to it at least seven times, if you are the average learner. Here are the rules of the game of *Incredible Recall.*

1. **Ready:** by pinpointing the likely exam item, term, definition or question, and isolate it from all others.

2. **Aim:** pull back the bow, and aim again and again until you get more consistently accurate. When you become skilled at recalling each item, you will be able to aim at the information and know that you will hit it before you have to "shoot" for it on the exam.

3. **Fire:** at the item before the exam and fire over and over and over until you KNOW that you can fire at the exam item and hit it without a doubt.

This sounds like more work than reading the textbook and your notes three times! It would be if we didn't have a streamlined system to shorten the time involved, one that accelerates your learning.

We have personally tested several sets of groups to see if using this method worked to any significant degree. We administered the same test to two classes on two different campuses who were accountable to learn the same information. We used identical multiple-choice exams on both campuses. On one campus we did not tell students about the method for internalizing information. On the other campus we drilled them in the use of the system until they used it on a regular basis.

In most of the experimental test classes, all but two or three students used the method faithfully. The average difference between the experimental and control (naïve) groups was about 12%. Which group do you suppose did better? Those who used the system. If you translate this percentage difference into grades, those students who used the method got a whole grade higher on their tests than those who did not use the method. A few students moved from "D's" on tests, to "B's", and still others went from "C's" to "A's".

We replicated this experiment three times with about the same results until we felt so guilty about not telling the students in the control (naïve) class that we had to stop using students as "guinea pigs" altogether. After students understand the system and try it, over 85% stick to it in their future courses.

It is Impossible to Read, Study and Recall *Everything!*

It is impossible for most people to read every word in every course that has assigned reading. And if they could, they likely couldn't memorize and recall all of it, unless they have photographic memories. Therefore, it is necessary to develop a system of *targeting* (setting up targets) for exam-related information. If you don't have targets on the "wall," you can't aim at them and hit any "bull's eyes." This is a MAJOR PROBLEM most people have when it comes to preparing for exams, writing papers effectively, and understanding what is required for success. Most students are not able to pinpoint what is likely to be on an exam, set it up separately as an exam item target, practice shooting at it, and learn to hit it consistently.

If you understand that your brain processes bite-sized information one bite at a time, you won't try to cram a whole pizza into it the night before an exam. Each "bite" must be cut, separated from the pizza, chewed, swallowed and digested before you get any food value out of it. If the piece of information is too big, you cannot go through this process.

Maximizing the Power of Note Card Technology

Extracting Bite Sized Chunks of Critically Relevant Information

Have you ever observed some students religiously summarizing course notes on small cards? You see their cards in their hands often, shuffling them, reviewing them, closing their eyes trying to remember their contents, and focused on the key learning topics stored on each of them. They may even have give you the stack to ask them questions. Did you ever realize that as you asked the questions, you yourself also learned? Have you ever noticed that these students generally do quite well on exams, are very efficient in their studying habits, are less stressed, happier, and perhaps more motivated about learning? Well, there is a reason: These students have developed a winning habit.

FRONT OF 3 X 5" NOTE CARD

Anomie

If you use the "technology" of managing information in small, bite-sized units, you will be able to isolate the information that is likely to be on an exam more efficiently. Once you extract the information from various sources, you can isolate it, rehearse it, test yourself and become competent to retrieve and apply that piece of information. This is, in a nutshell, the way you study for a multiple-choice exam. The extra bonus benefit is that once you can master the information at the retrieval level, then you can put the pieces of it together into meaningful essays on essay exams. Here is an example of how a note card can be used to memorize a term in a textbook or a lecture. Write the term you want to memorize on the front of the card...and write the definition of it on the back.

How to Use Note Card Technology

Follow the steps below to increase your scores on exams.

READY! Start targeting for exam items as early and consistently as possible. The earlier and more frequently you make cards, the more time you have for rehearsing and practice shooting.

1. Do not study the cards while you are making them, just make them quickly.
2. Make a card for anything you think might show up on an exam.
3. Don't worry about learning at this point; all you are trying to do is get likely targets identified - terms, concepts, definitions, studies, authors, and so on - that are likely to be on exams.
4. When in doubt, make a note card and place it in the stack with the others for that chapter of your textbook or lecture session. If the textbook chapter and the lecture go together, then put them in the same pile.
5. Put a rubber band around all the cards for that chapter and lecture.
6. Label the course name and chapter number on the front card in the deck.
7. Be very fast. You will complete a chapter faster than reading it. You will have scanned the whole chapter very fast from a strategic point of view toward extracting critically exam-relevant data. Then you can more wisely go back and read key parts of the chapters later.

Usually you will make a note card for the following items in the text and from the lecture:

- All bold or italicized words that introduce new terms, with their definitions on the back of the card.
- If the instructor says, "This will be on the exam," then make a note card (MNC).

- If the instructor gets excited about something or emphasizes it, then he or she will likely remember to put it on an exam, so MNC.
- If another student says to you, "This issue was on the exam last year," then MNC.
- If you find last year's exam in the library and the instructor is still using the same textbook, then, MNC.
- MNC for important research results on one side, author on the other side of the card.
- Check with other students in your class who are making note cards to see if they have cards that you do not.
- Borrow cards from students who made note cards last year and ask them to put a red mark on the ones that they remember with certainty were on the exam.
- Some professors give students study guidelines or hints in order to assist them in exam preparation - MNC.
- Make note cards: MNC.
- Make note cards: MNC.
- Make note cards: MNC.

By now, you are likely getting the idea that we are suggesting that you use note cards to organize, manage, target, rehearse and get skilled at retrieving information. This works great for learning a foreign language too!

AIM! After You Get Your Deck of Cards Made

Read your text book chapter quickly and notice how many of the terms you are already familiar with! You will be amazed at how many you remember.

1. If you are a kinesthetic learner, you have already made something happen with information, like transferring it from one place on a page to another place on a note card, which has helped you to learn.
2. If you are an auditory learner, then say out loud what is on the card.
3. If you are a social learner, then flash card your friends in groups. Have a serious group-grope flash card party.
4. If you are a cognitive learner, then review your note cards alone.

5. Any card that you are 100% confident that you could ACE on a test, place in the KNOW pile and set it to the side.
6. Any card that you aren't sure of, place it in the DON'T KNOW pile and set it aside.
7. Continue to go through the DON'T KNOW pile until all of the cards end up in the KNOW pile! Usually, you will be able to recall most all of them after a maximum of seven or eight repetitions. Then you will be a state of CLEAR. That's when all your cards are in the KNOW pile and your desk is CLEAR!

There! Voilá! You just tested yourself over and over again really fast so that you know that you know!

Anxiety level down. Retention up. Confidence up. Go play! Celebrate. Read your textbook again and notice how much you know now! You will be amazed at how knowledgeable you are.

If your professor pulls a trick on you, like one of ours did on one of us, she might change her mind and give you an essay exam instead of a multiple-choice one. Did that author care? NOT. He had a pile of facts and terms to weave into interesting answers fast. He built an outline, and started writing. He went from getting "C's" and "B's" to getting "A's" in less than a month. He spent over 30% less time staring blankly at a text book page because he was on data overload, and arrived at state of "CLEAR" in less time than ever.

Go blow away the exam: ***FIRE!***

Other Uses of Note Cards

Note cards are handy. When you put rubber bands around them, they are distinct piles of information you can use to prepare for exams, or to write papers. (Our students successfully quote instructors in their papers by making note cards of what he or she says during lectures).

You can use note cards to write down quotes from library books or journal articles in the library and put all the bibliographic information on the back of the card. When it comes time to organize your paper, you are ready.

Put all of the headings and topics you want to cover in your paper on note cards, including the ones you got from the library, your text, from the lecture, on the floor, or on a presentation board or wall. Arrange them into an outline. Move them around until you find just the right order of ideas, and then enter them into your word processor in that order. How about that for creative flow and logical chutzpa!

We saw one student who, after he caught onto this idea, went berserk with technology and bought one of those little hand scanners and plugged it into his portable computer. He scanned things out of his textbook, out of library books, and typed notes from the lecture. Then he organized all this information in his word processing program, printed the information out as note cards for use in serious group flashing, and later used the information to write essays and papers and to complete related work on projects. Sharp nerd. He became a party animal in his newly-found spare time.

Use note cards to internalize, organize and store information that is personally interesting. After you are satisfied that you are winning The Game, you can use note cards to keep track of very interesting information that you personally never want to forget. One of us has kept over 4000 such note cards that he has entered into his computer. Interesting sayings. Mind-blowing learning he never wants to forget. Stuff he wants to include in his next book, and so on.

After you have rehearsed for your exam so that you know that you know, there are still some powerful strategies that can raise your scores on various types of exams. These strategies are outlined below.

Get Ready For Different Kinds of Exams

Additional Strategies for Acing Multiple Choice or True-False Exams

1. Make sure that you read the question very carefully. Slow down your usual rate of reading and double-check to insure that you truly understand the question.

2. Answer all the questions you are confident about first.

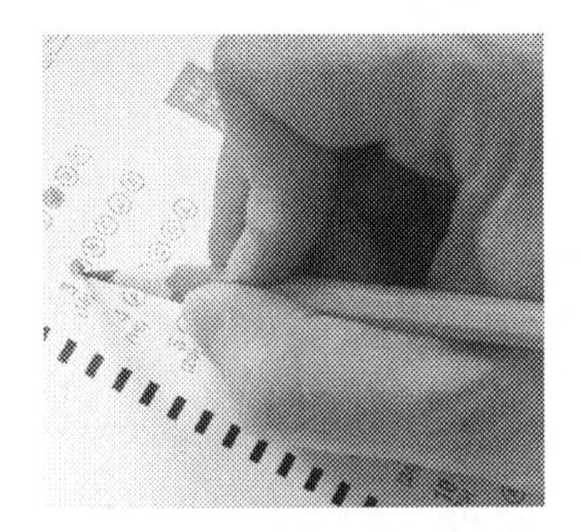

3. Skip the ones you aren't sure of, and come back to them.

4. Cross out answers that you know are incorrect before you mark the answer you think is correct.

5. Answer every question unless your professor informs you that you will lose points for wrong answers.

6. After you finish the exam, go over the whole thing again, and double-check your answers.

7. Don't change any answers unless you are confident that your first answer was incorrect. Research has shown that your first response is more often correct than your second, revised response.

8. Choose the best answer available - not every question will have answers that are "right on." If you have extra time, maximize your chances of getting the right answer by doing some of the following:

   - Read the question and see how it fits with each answer by rereading the question each time you consider an optional answer.
   - Supply your own answer before you look at the answers provided and see which one comes the closest to your answer.
   - When you are unsure, choose answers that have adjectives in the sentences such as, most often, usually, probably.
   - Steer away from answers that have words in them such as only, never, always, everyone, or totally.
   - Consider that in most objective exams the first answer is the one that is least likely to be correct. Instructors think that if they put the correct answer first, they are "giving it away."

Additional Strategies for Acing Short Answer Exams

1. Make sure that the answer you give makes logical and grammatical sense – double check this.

2. Write the first answer or answers that come to your mind lightly in pencil in the left or right hand margin before you decide what the correct answer really is. After you think about it and feel resolved, come back to the question and write in your well-considered answer.

3. More than one word may be required when filling in each blank. Fill in several words when appropriate, unless you have been told to insert only one word.

4. Note that the structure of the sentence forces certain kinds of correct answers, such as "A ________________ will get you nowhere fast." The correct response must start with a consonant, not a vowel. If your choices are "ailing auto" and "broken bicycle," your choice is clear. The correct words are, "broken bicycle." A dead giveaway. When the missing word must start with a vowel it is even more of a gift!

Specific Strategies for Dealing with Matching Questions

1. Read both columns so your brain has a chance to get the bigger picture.
2. Start with the test items that are the easiest for you. Take the easiest item in the left hand column and scan the right hand column for a match.
3. Cross out each item that you have used.

Strategies for Dealing with Essay Exams

1. Before you start writing, read all of the test questions.
2. Divide the total amount of time you have on the exam equally between questions. Give yourself a limit for each question so you don't get behind and have unanswered questions at the end of the exam. If you run out of time, during the last few minutes, make an outline of what you would have written.
3. Start writing on the topic for which you are most sure that you have correct, thorough and creative answers.
4. Write in a double-spaced format so that your professor won't get a headache reading the essay, and use extra space between questions in case you want to add points later.
5. Before you start writing, build a mini-outline on a separate piece of paper that will provide you with some logical structure for your essay.
6. Introduce each of your answers with a sentence that summarizes what you are going to say.
7. Build in evidence to support each point that you are making.
8. Make smooth transitions from one section of the essay to the next to help your instructor follow the train of your thoughts.
9. Proof your essay for errors or wrong information.
10. Correct spelling, punctuation, and grammatical errors.
11. Add any other points that come to mind at the bottom of the page, on another page, or on the back of the page, but show where the point belongs in the context of your essay by using an asterisk.

Chapter Three

Research, Structure, Write and Edit a Paper

If what you're working for really matters, you'll give it all you've got.
NIDO QUBEIN

Introduction

In this chapter you will gain an overview of the main considerations for producing a quality paper that will help you reach your goals of getting the grades you want. It will also help you to organize your learning so that it "sticks" and becomes useful to you in the future.

Writing at the University Level

Why is writing at university different? If you are a student just coming out of high school and are looking at writing your first essay or term paper, there are terms and phrases that are likely very foreign to you. High school essays are not the same as those required at the post-secondary level and have elements that many high school curricula have not covered.

Writing at the university level is not necessarily harder than what you may have done in the past, but there are different elements that must be included in your assignment in order to meet the academic requirements and prepare you for future papers in higher-level courses. This chapter is designed to help first-year and returning students with the basic elements for writing a term paper or essay, and can be expanded on by utilizing other writing guides or accessing the writing resource centre at your institution.

Consider Your Audience

When writing at the first-year level, there is more to writing a paper than your opening paragraph, body, and closing paragraph. Before thinking about how to structure your paper and write your outline, the first element that must be addressed is your **audience**. Who are you writing this paper for? Does your reader understand the topic you are writing about? Are you writing for someone who is familiar with your subject matter or for the general public? These are questions that may already have been answered by your instructor or professor in the assignment instructions, but if these questions are unclear, ask for clarification. Perhaps, most importantly, if you are writing a paper for a particular professor, you want to know exactly what is expected if you are to do well.

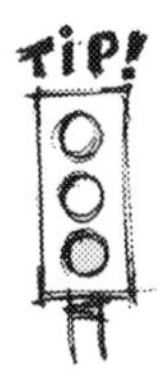

Major Paper Writing Success Tip: Since most of the time your audience will be your professor; you will want to find out exactly what your professors' expectations are for each assignment. If you fulfill these expectations, the grades you will receive on your paper will be higher. If you fail to understand a particular professor's expectations, your grade will suffer. This is significant when you consider that in most courses your written assignments count for 40%-60% of your final grade. Whenever possible, get the professors to be as specific as possible in telling you what they are looking for. If they won't tell you, find a student who had a previous class with that professor and received and A, and ask them if you can see their paper!

Specifically, you should know the following points about an assignment before you start writing:

1. The purpose of the assignment;

2. What you are supposed to demonstrate that you have learned from the assignment;
3. The points that you are expected to cover in your paper;
4. The number of references you are expected to have researched or read and quoted in your paper;
5. The required page length of the assignment;
6. The style sheet you are expected to use for the assignment (the layout and formatting of the document, such as APA, etc.);
7. What an "A" paper looks like! If you can see a graded paper that your professor has marked, then you will gain great insight into what you would have to do in order to be that successful!

A good rule of thumb for first-year papers is to write your paper as if your audience is **not** familiar with your subject matter, as it will demonstrate to your instructor that you understand your subject matter and can clearly articulate your **thesis** statement or main argument.

The second element in considering your audience is to make it clear to your reader **why** you are writing about this topic or subject. Is this an explanation of a phenomenon or behaviour? Are you reviewing available information on the subject? Or are you identifying new avenues for research into the causes or effects of your chosen topic? The greatest difficulty in writing a paper is lack of clarity about the purpose or requirements of an assignment. As a student, you may discover that many instructors or professors are not completely clear about the intent of a particular written assignment themselves. Knowing the purpose and requirements of an assignment will help you focus your efforts, so that you can earn a higher grade and learn more at the same time.

It is not enough to simply provide information on a subject or topic without having a purpose for it. Explanations of an incident are welcome, but at the university level there is an expectation of some degree of analysis of the phenomenon, incident, or topic that you are writing about. Tell the reader why you are examining this information and what you wish for your reader to learn. Then provide references to others who have researched or written about the subject so that you can demonstrate that you have considered multiple points of view and have arrived at a tentative critical perspective.

Papers without a purpose are BORING. They go nowhere, don't grab the reader, and don't impress the instructor, who may actually not enjoy reading them. A paper engages our attention only when its contents might make some kind of informative difference to the reader(s). Understanding the purpose of the assignment involves answering the question of why the instructor, or you, wants this assignment written. Once you can pinpoint this purpose, you can get a bead on a target that will help you succeed. An example of a paper with a purpose is as follows:

> *This paper will enable readers to better examine various ways of knowing anything. The study of various ways of knowing is called epistemology. Once you understand the various ways of knowing, you will be better able to determine why you assume certain things to be true. As a result, you will then gain perspective on why you believe what you do in regards to philosophy, religion and spiritual matters. The more you can pinpoint what ways of knowing that you believe to be valid, the more sure you can be about knowing anything with confidence. This paper will present a summary of these ways of knowing, assist you to choose which ways you believe have credence, and clarify what you believe to be true based on your new understanding of epistemology.*

Now, would you want to read this paper if you were searching to understand the meaning of life? Probably you would. Therefore, the point is to write something that you are interested in, for readers who will likely have an interest.

Thesis, Hypothesis, or Question

What is the main question, thesis statement, or hypothesis that sets out the plan for the discussion in your paper? This is where some of the terms and elements required at the university level which may not have been identified in high school begin to appear.

Thesis statement

This is the main idea or position the writer takes and is explaining to his or her reader on a given subject or topic. Often this statement is in the first or second paragraph of the paper or essay, and informs the reader what subject or topic the writer is discussing, what opinion or position the writer is taking on the subject (do you approve or disapprove? Agree or disagree?), and how the writer is planning to make this argument (through critical analysis, case study, or examination through a theoretical perspective).

Hypothesis

A hypothesis is a question that the writer is attempting to answer about a topic, subject, or phenomenon. The writer's research - as shown in the body of the paper - will either support or disprove his or her proposed answer, which then forms the basis for the **conclusion** of the paper.

Nearly every paper, essay, or article at the university level must have a thesis statement or hypothesis clearly articulated or explained at the beginning of the paper. This does not necessarily have to be the first sentence of the paper, but **must** be clear within the first one or two paragraphs

Thinking and Writing Critically to Demonstrate You can be Objective

One of the complaints that companies and employers have of recent university graduates is that they lack critical analysis skills (Hansen and Hansen, n.d.), and yet many universities state that this is one of the key competencies their departments are teaching their students.

Critical analysis is the ability to look at a topic, subject, theory, or any piece of information and break it down into key components to be able to determine what it actually means in an objective way. Does it make sense? What are the positives and negatives associated with it? Are there flaws in the author's arguments or errors in the research methodologies used? You must also be able to determine whether you as a researcher agree with it, agree with it in some aspects but not in others, disagree with it in this instance, or disagree with it in its entirety. If you disagree, you have to present evidence to the contrary and not just say you disagree. You are not required to agree with the opposite perspective; however, you must be able to understand it, explain it, and acknowledge it. Critical analysis, then, is most simply understood as being able to view and examine both sides of your argument, and then come to a reasoned but tentative conclusion based upon the evidence that you have examined thus far.

What critical analysis does **not** involve is emotions or value judgments; a critical analysis does not imply - or state - to the reader that you value one perspective over the other. Academic writing strives to be value- and judgement-free in its examination of an issue. The writer is welcome to discuss the feelings about the topic as held by other individuals, but the writer must not use what are termed value laden words, or words that evoke an **emotional response** in the reader.

You as the author can state your own personal opinion(s) in the conclusion of your paper but clearly identify them as such and reserve them for the end of your paper. In fact, some professors give you points for expressing your own views and ideas... but others may dock you points for stating your personal opinion. Thus, we can see another reason why it is important to understand your professor's expectations before you start writing an assignment.

Examples of value laden words include such terms as "monstrous" or "heinous" to describe a person accused of a crime. These examples are easily found in newspaper articles and on television news broadcasts. If a term you are planning to use in your paper is one that may give away how you personally feel about your subject or discussion, the best remedy is to change it or delete it entirely. To find more information on critical thinking, you can go to this web site for further insight: **http://www.criticalthinking.org/aboutCT/definingCT.shtml**.

Stating an Opinion without Emotion in Order to Demonstrate you Can Remain Objective and Open-minded

So how do you write a paper that asks you to give your opinion about a topic without giving away your gut feelings? This is a difficult goal that most new writers must learn to achieve. When writing a paper that involves a critical analysis, or any submission at the university level, the writer must evaluate the subject matter on its own merits. Questions you might ask yourself are: How has this subject or topic been evaluated by past researchers or theorists? Are there any prior criticisms? Have you come up with new criticisms or new ways in which it is appropriate? Or is it simply a case of whether or not the explanation, theory, or subject "works"?

Academic writing is about attempting to remove as much personal bias from the subject matter as possible and examine it in an objective fashion. Some researchers argue that there is no truly objective research (Pfohl, 1994); however, in the interest of the scientific method, we do the best that we can. By staying away from emotional or value laden language, new writers are on the right path to learning how to write at an academic level.

Writing Your Paper

Start with an Outline

In every first-year class that requires a paper or essay assignment, the best advice we as educators can give our students in writing their first papers is to work from an outline. An outline is the easiest and most effective way for a writer to stay on track with the subject matter and any discussions about it that are to be presented to the reader. The outline also provides you with a skeleton that is a solid logical framework to organize all of the material for your paper. Your outline can also verify that you will cover all of the required points for a successful assignment.

The outline is the basic framework of your article or assignment, and works for assignments as small as a news-style article and as large as a Master's level thesis or PhD dissertation. Some instructors even require their students to produce an outline as part of the assignment itself.

Creation of an outline starts very simply, and can become as complex as the writer wishes. Some outlines may be as simple as a title, thesis statement, main argument(s), and conclusion. Others may use these as headings under which more specific phrases, sentences, or even quoted and paraphrased references may be listed. It depends on how much guidance the writer feels is necessary in composing the work. As an example, for this very chapter, we created a very specific outline with headings covering each aspect of the writing process we wished to address for students and the specific information that we felt was most important to convey before starting to write any of the paragraphs of the chapter. Clear section headings and subheadings are the key to building a strong framework from which to write a solid paper.

The note cards that you created to help you study can help you at this stage, too. After you have clarified the purpose and requirements for your paper, you are ready to build your first outline. Most of the headings you see in this book were first created as notes of ideas we had about what we believed to be most important in each chapter. After we did our research and reviewed other possible topics that we should include, we changed the outline. You can always change the outline! If you have taken notes from lectures, kept note cards of various interesting ideas you've had, and note cards on the requirements you are supposed to cover for the assignment, you can arrange these note cards in a logical order and enter them into a word processor.

An outline is also like having a road map to follow from the beginning to the end of the writing process, as it provides you not only with the starting and end points of your writing destination, but all the "sights" you wish to stop at along the way. Doing the outline forces you to get clear about what directions you should go when you go to the library to do research on what others have written on this topic.

Outlines also provide opportunities for fine-tuning or editing some of the major components of the paper prior to writing them fully. Writing the outline allows the writer to look at the skeleton of the paper and see if there is something that does not quite fit with the rest of the work. By seeing any flaws that immediately stand out, the writer is able to conduct additional research to explain the error or flaw, and determine whether it should be included in the work, excluded as a mistake, included as a sub-topic, or as an avenue for further research.

In later years of undergraduate work, graduate, or post-graduate studies, outlines take on the new term of research proposals. These can be similar to term papers in themselves, but likely also cannot be written without the aid of an outline. Even an outline may need an outline.

Most word processing programs have an outline feature built into the software program that can save you a huge amount of time in the long run. It is a great idea to take a course that teaches you to take advantage of the powerful features that the word processor that you plan to use has built into it. Also, turn on your spell checker, grammar checker, and other helpful tools so that you can have technology working on your side while you write!

Do Your Initial Library Research and Literature Review

Use your outline to guide your library research. After you have become clear about the assignment, its purpose and requirements, and have built an initial rough outline, it is important to take the next step and go to the library. Many students try to avoid the library like the plague because they feel overwhelmed by the immensity of it, don't know how to use the computer terminals to access information, or don't want to appear "stupid." Librarians are there to help people learn how to access various resources in the library, so don't hesitate to ask for help. One invaluable resource cherished by researchers is the on-line catalogue of databases available at each library. They are massive. In fact, if you look hard enough, you can often find the original text for most research papers, journal articles, books, theses, and dissertations. These resources not only provide access to a large body of peer-reviewed, credible work done by others, citing them can also impress many instructors, because it will indicate that you made an effort to find credible information to support your paper. Best of all, you don't even need to leave your couch to look for the information you need! The vast majority of anything you will ever need is available on-line either through your City or college library. This is diametrically different from yesteryears, where many of us had to physically go the library each time we needed access to resource materials. So, enjoy!

Use your chapter title and headings as guides to help you look up various other works, journals, books, or magazines by title. If you already know an author, it can be made even simpler. Search for the most likely resources that will amplify your key points or support your position. Learn as much as you can about others who have explored things from your point of view and quote them in your paper as important validation.

Search for resources that support the opposing position. It will help you get a higher grade on your paper if you can present both sides, or present more than two or three perspectives. Your professors will be more impressed if you can compare and contrast several perspectives.

Check your resources out of the library, or create note cards of the quotes you want to use before leaving. Note cards will help you to carefully place your quotes in strategic places of your paper where they will count the most, be the most logically supportive of your position (or thesis) and have the most impact. Remember, your note cards can be especially valuable when you prepare for an essay examination, especially when they contain rich resources to quote in an essay question.

Use the photocopier to record bibliographic information and quotes when a page or more is important for you to take from the library. This can be expensive but can save you much time and energy in checking out a pile of books, many of which you may not use in the end.

Complete the literature review. You can use these main sources of information to review the book and journal literature that may be relevant to your topic. This review can constitute a separate summary of the literature, which some instructors or professors do require. Completing this step proves that you are capable of doing a thorough review of the perspectives that may be relevant to support or challenge your position in your paper or thesis. Completing this literature review is hard evidence to your instructor that you "ain't no indelicacy slob," when it comes to gaining an overview of alternative or conflicting points of view. It can be fun to see trends or conflicts in the research or theoretical developments in your area of interest.

Refine Your Outline and Integrate Your Resources

Organize the main points of your paper into a more refined outline of note cards and photocopied resources. This will help you to refine your thinking and will give your paper a sense of flow.

Enter the headings and resources from your refined outline (the new sequence you have designed on note cards) into your word processor in the new sequence you have developed. This is where you can do some expanding and rearranging so that your whole paper hangs together, is more interesting and has impact in accomplishing its purpose.

Take advantage of the outlining, spell-checking and thesaurus options of your word processing program. Be patient and use them creatively to refine your paper into a high quality presentation. Using these powerful tools can be fun. It will also give your paper that extra "punch" it might need to score a few extra points. This can mean one higher grade on your paper - and this can mean a higher grade in the course.

Ensure that you use footnotes properly, according to the style sheet required by your teacher. Ask for a sample of style sheet requirements so that you can double check your formats against those required.

Print your first rough draft and edit it yourself. It is important that you go through this step on your own. It will make you realize that your paper is written in your own "blood" and that it is truly yours. When you go on to the next step of having someone else read and edit it, you may feel that they are criticizing you personally, to some extent. Don't perceive the criticism that way, but view it as a necessary part of the process to get an "A" or "B" on your paper.

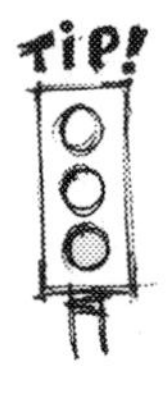

Have someone who is knowledgeable about writing, and who knows the subject you are writing about, proof your paper for grammatical, punctuation, and syntax errors, and have her or him critique your paper's impact, depth and meaning. If you can find two or three people to give you this feedback, you will be even further ahead. It won't take you much time to have others read your paper and write some "red line" suggestions to improve your paper. These suggestions will be especially valuable if your readers are experienced or understand the requirements of your instructor when it comes time to grade your paper.

Insert the changes recommended by your editor(s) into your document using your word processor. This stage is your last chance to make some serious last minute revisions.

Complete a final spell check. This step is important because you have likely made a number of revisions or added text that you have not spell-checked yet. This step may take less than one minute, but speaks loudly when your instructor cannot find any spelling errors in your paper.

You Gotta Have Style

Another important question that students should ask their instructors or professors, if it is not already clearly stated, is which layout and referencing **style** they should use. A style refers to the method and template for indicating which sources of information the writer has utilized both in the body and at the end of the paper, and how the paper should be laid out in terms of margins and table placement.

There are numerous styles available to students, and many of these choices are at the discretion of your institution, department, or instructor or professor, including:

- APA style (American Psychological Association) - psychology, social sciences
- ASA style (American Sociological Association) - sociology, social sciences
- MLA style (Modern Languages Association) - arts and humanities, English, Communications
- Chicago or Turabian styles (foot- or endnote styles) - arts and humanities

Most university departments or schools will clearly indicate in their information which style of referencing they prefer. Check with your department head or program assistant if there is a particular requirement at your institution.

Where Do I Find Information on Style?

Most organizations with particular styles have been very progressive with creating websites with very specific examples for writers to be able to follow their guides. TheAPA style guide can be found at **www.apastyle.org**, ASA at **www.asanet.org**, MLA at **www.mla.org**, and Chicago style at **www.chicagomanualofstyle.org**. Turabian style - developed by Kate Turabian, dissertation secretary at the University of Chicago (The University of Chicago Press, 2006) - is closely associated with Chicago style and can be easily located on several university writing guide websites, such as Ohio State University's (2005) "Research and Internet Guides and Tools" page, at **www.lib.ohio-state.edu/sites/guides/turabiangd.html**.

Check your university or local bookstore as well. Most common styles mentioned above were available in book formats long before the internet came along. Students can easily pick up from their university bookstore a writing guide that covers several of the most commonly-used styles, or books on the specific styles themselves. These books are also available for purchase online from the organizations themselves or other online booksellers such as Chapters/Indigo and Amazon.

Should I Use In-Text or Noted Citations?

This choice is again at the discretion of your instructor or professor, and while it is best to become familiar with both methods of citing sources, most first-year courses will prefer students to use in-text citations in their assignments.

Footnotes and endnotes are more commonly used in scientific disciplines, but are also available in other styles. APA style more often allows the use of endnotes or footnotes where there is information provided in the assignment that does not necessarily fit into the paper or is a "tangent" (Online Writing Lab at Purdue University, 2004) and the author must provide a **brief** summary or explanation for its inclusion. If the explanation is longer than a few sentences covering **one** idea, it is recommended to be included in an *appendix*[1].

References

Make sure that you have consulted your style guide to determine how you should format your list of references that are included at the end of your assignment. Even if you only have one source that you have used in your paper, you must include it on a list. Different styles have different titles or names for this list, and it is most important to ensure that you are using the correct title. APA style requires this list to be titled "References", while MLA and Chicago styles both call it a "Works Cited" list.

Do not use "Bibliography" as the title for your sources list as the term refers to **every** article, book, paper, or essay ever written on your subject. As this would be largely impossible to compile even in a PhD dissertation, stick to what your style tells you.

Your list of sources is to include every source **cited** or referenced in your paper or assignment. If you did not use the source, do not include it in your list. Also be aware that if there is a source cited in your paper that is **not** included in your list, it may cast suspicion upon you regarding possible plagiarism or *Academic Dishonesty*.

The growth of the internet and available software has made referencing your sources as simple as conducting online research now. Websites such as RefWorks (**www.refworks.com**) provide students with access through their library websites to use their software to enable them to select their online source for inclusion in a

[1]*Appendices are covered later in this chapter.*

personal online database of resources. With just a few mouse clicks, students can produce a list of references that can be cut-and-pasted into their existing document, all following the required style.

I Think My Appendix Just Burst

An appendix - or appendices, plural - is included in the paper after your list of sources in accordance with APA style (Ibid.). An appendix may include a table of results or figures, a copy of a survey questionnaire, its coding sheet, or even a short newspaper, magazine, or internet article that is referenced or cited in the assignment but the reader may not have seen.

Separate appendices are used for each article, table, or document to be attached to the assignment, and are listed as "Appendix A," "Appendix B," and so forth (without the quotations, of course).

For a first-year class, one can generally use the rule that if it is important to your paper, and cannot be explained in a footnote, you may include each article as an appendix.

Do I Need a Table of Contents?

Again, this is another element that is at the discretion of your teacher, but generally - and check with your instructor **just to be sure** - if your paper is less than twenty pages, you likely will not need a table of contents. Short assignments about simple topics or subjects will not have as many sections as will a research study or literature review, and as such will not need to have the sections of the paper identified.

If your paper is long enough, or if you are required to include a table of contents, most word processing programs have menu functions to automatically compile and update a table of contents as the paper is edited. Microsoft Word uses formatted headings to construct tables of contents and is very easy to use.

Most universities have writing centres or resource staff available in the library to provide help for students writing papers and assignments and can assist with the creation of tables of contents. Most word processors have the capability of generating a table of contents automatically if you use the outlining feature of the program.

Tables of contents are **not** included in your final page count, even if your word processor recognizes it as page one or page two.

Title Pages

Once again, different instructors have different ways in which they want you to construct the title page for your assignment, but if this has not been clearly stated, the title and subtitle (if any) should be centred in the middle of the page (or slightly higher than the middle). Identifying information including your name, student number, course name and section number, name of your instructor and teaching assistant (if any) are located at the bottom right-hand corner and may be aligned to the right margin.

Unless you have been given permission to do so, academic papers are **not** to include pictures, graphics, watermark effects, clip art or images of any kind on the title page. Submissions to academic journals, societies, and such do not accept clip art or other images on title pages. It may seem plain and boring, but such additions are distracting to the reader, especially one who is grading your assignment.

Title pages also do not include the following items or characteristics:

- headers or footers
- page numbers
- the file pathway where your paper is saved on your computer

To keep your title page from interfering with your table of contents or word count feature, you can create the title page as a separate document. Save this document as a template and you will never again wonder how to create a title page for future assignments as it will all be there.

Headers and Footers

Typically in undergraduate papers, the only thing to be included in the margin space of your paper is your page number. Unless specified, the page number is most commonly located in the **bottom right-hand corner** of the footer on each page.

Your name, course name and section, instructor name, and other such information are already present on your title page, and do not need to be included in either the headers or footers of your pages.

Font Size, Type, Margins, and Spacing

Font Size and Type

Even though there are almost literally zillions of fonts available out on the Internet and built into our word processing programs, it is not appropriate to use them all in academic writing. Again, it seems plain and boring, but most often the fonts and sizes that will be accepted in academic assignments are Times New Roman font at twelve-point and Arial font at 11-point. The reason for using these fonts is that there is evidence that readers move faster through serif-type fonts (like this Baskerville font you are reading here) and retain more of what they have read than other types, because "serif fonts have markings that make rows of text appear to set on a line" (Gasser, Boeke, Hafferman, & Tan, 2005, p. 185). Newspapers often use these fonts for the same reason... most people are comfortable with and expect them.

Your instructor, professor, or even teaching assistant may specify certain fonts and sizes to be used, or may simply reject fonts that are too fancy, too big, too narrow, or too childish-looking. Often the best way to go is with your software default font. Fonts that are too fancy-looking may be far too difficult to read and will not gain you extra points for presentation.

As well, do not reduce or enlarge your font as a way to ensure that you meet your minimum or maximum page requirement. The person grading your paper will recognize this tactic and it may mean the difference between an A or a B.

Ensure that you remove any "hyperlinks" (Internet addresses) and underlining in your citations or references and change to black text when you are printing your document. Hyperlinks are pointless if you are submitting a hard copy.

Coloured text, fancy paper, and elaborate presentation covers and bindings - unless requested - make it look like you are trying too hard to get a good grade or are trying to hide a bad paper in a nice cover.

Keep it simple and staple your paper in the top left-hand corner. Many dollar stores have small staplers available for a dollar or less, or find a stapler in the computer lab printing area, photocopy room, or a reception desk. Some students develop elaborate methods of folding and tearing the top left corners of their papers to keep them together when handing them in, but this only serves to make your paper look like it has been damaged or that you did not care about its presentation. Paperclips are also not advisable, as they may fall off or cause parts of your paper to become attached to the paper of another student.

Margins for Error

Once again the default settings in your word processing program are going to be adequate for your paper. Most often these settings are 1.0 inches for the top and bottom margins (to accommodate the headers and footers), and 1.0 to 1.25 inches for the right and left margins.

Your instructor can use the margin space to add comments or suggest edits or other information in the grading process to help you become a better writer. Changing these settings to achieve your page count is also not a good idea, as the person grading your paper will see it as laziness and avoiding learning how to properly format and edit an assignment.

Line, Please

Lines and paragraphs for academic submissions - including theses and dissertations - are always double-spaced. It is not only easier to read and provides more space for your instructor space for grading, but when it comes to more formal assignments or academic submissions, there is room for a proof-reader or editor to make comments, suggestions, and edits.

There is also not an extra space between paragraphs, even though we have done so in this textbook. The first line of each new paragraph is to be indented at one inch - word processing programs can be set to do this automatically - and serves to indicate where the new paragraph starts.

Again, do not reduce or increase your line spacing in order to fit your page count. Better to learn how to edit than face the red ink!

Short Forms: Abbreviations, Acronyms, and Contractions

Abbreviations

Make sure you understand where and when an abbreviation is appropriate and whether or not you are using it correctly.

When using "i.e." or "e.g.," the easiest way to understand these abbreviations is that "i.e." is similar to the phrase "that is," while "e.g." is similar to "for example". If you are not sure which one is appropriate, check with your writing centre or choose not to use them; instead, use a full phrase to indicate what it is you mean.

"Et. al." refers to the Latin term *et alia* meaning "and others" and is used in in-text citations, endnotes, or footnotes where there are more than three authors listed for a source. In your list of sources, "et. al." is not allowed. Instead, list all the authors for the source.

"Ibid." or *ibidem* is another Latin term meaning "in the same place" and may be used in APA style only when making a reference to the **same source** which immediately preceded it.

"Etc." or "et cetera" is another Latin term also translated to "and the others" and is often seen in lists of items. This is considered in academic writing to be a *colloquialism*[2] and is to be avoided at all costs.

If you are ever in doubt when you are allowed to use an abbreviation or which abbreviation is appropriate, ask your instructor or teaching assistant for assistance.

Acronyms

Acronyms are allowed in academic writing, but the writer must use the full name of the organization, statute or legislation, province, state, or company **first**. If you are using an acronym in subsequent references to something that commonly uses an acronym, you must include it in parentheses following the first usage of the full name, e.g. Servants Anonymous Society (SAS).

If you are using an acronym to refer to a governmental statute, law, or piece of legislation, remember that statutes must either be underlined or *italicized* in both their full form and in the acronym itself, e.g. *Youth Criminal Justice Act (YCJA).*

Acronyms or abbreviations that are used informally by professors or teaching assistants in lecture or classes are often encountered by students; however, they are considered to be "jargon" that not everyone will be familiar with. For example, in criminology, many instructors refer to the criminal justice system as the "cjs" and many students assume that this is an acceptable abbreviation. While an instructor, teaching assistant, or another criminology student will understand what is meant by this abbreviation, anyone else outside of this field may not be familiar with the term, and as such it is not allowed in academic writing.

I'm Having Contractions!

Contractions are also not allowed in academic writing; therefore, students should get used to using longer forms instead of contractions. Exceptions to this rule include direct quotations, titles, headings (as in this very chapter), and proper nouns such as the name of a company, e.g. "It's Just Lunch" (It's Just Lunch, 2006).

[2] *Refers to informal speech.*

A popular misuse is the possessive form "its" versus the contraction "it's". "Its" refers to the possessive of "it" when gender is not indicated as in the case of an inanimate object or an animal whose gender is not known. "It's" is a contraction for "it is" and is therefore not allowed in formal academic writing.

Making Your Paper Look Fine

Print a second draft

What? You mean I have to read this paper again?! Yes, one more time, to find those little errors that show up in how your paper is laid out, how the page breaks occur, and how it looks, overall. Trust us! You most likely will find errors in a document that appeared to be just perfect on the computer monitor! Get used to correcting errors...every professor or instructor will be very impressed when you submit a paper that is virtually error free... and the grade you get on the paper will usually be higher as a result.

Make sure that you have told your word processor to automatically break the pages in the correct spots to keep headings with the text below it. If the headings and text don't stay together, you can force them to by placing a page break after the text, or before the heading yourself. See your word processor manual to see how to do this. It isn't difficult.

Print the final draft

Print this final draft on higher quality paper, if possible. You aren't trying to make a status statement at this time, but trying to get your paper to stand out from the rest a little bit. Don't use fibrous paper, but smooth, "matte" paper designed for printing on laser or dot matrix printers. If the style sheet allows, use the Times New Roman font style. Do not justify the right margin; leave it ragged. It is easier to read. Instructors are used to reading this font because it is quite often selected for books.

This is the time everything can go wrong. Your word processor freezes up, you lose all your formatting, your printer ribbon or laser printer drum go dry, you lose your backup disk and your hard disk crashes, and you wish you could throw in the towel and quit life. KEEP TWO BACKUP COPIES in two different places so that you minimize the possibility that your work could be lost. If your instructor loses your paper, you will have to print out another copy of it. Keep all your notes and note cards, as well. If, for some reason, you lose all your electronic records, you will have to reconstruct your paper from your notes.

That's Cheating!

Academic dishonesty and plagiarism are two very problematic issues faced by universities and post-secondary institutions today.

Most universities provide definitions and policies in their student handbooks and course calendars regarding academic dishonesty. University of the Fraser Valley (UFV) in British Columbia and Northern Alberta Institute of Technology (NAIT) include plagiarism and cheating as part of their policy regarding academic misconduct or dishonesty that and may be committed intentionally or unintentionally. Basically, most post secondary institutions define cheating as presenting someone else work in part or full as you own. Forgetting to include a citation, unintentionally copying, or otherwise misleading the reader into believing that the article or essay is the author's own original work are all examples of plagiarism. Check your institution's website or calendar for the academic dishonesty policies.

How Did You Know?

It is actually quite easy to determine whether or not a portion of, or a whole essay or assignment, has not been written by the author identified on the title page. Some instructors and teaching assistants use such websites as Turn It In (**www.turnitin.com**), and My Drop Box (**www.mydropbox.com**) - both of which are integrated with WebCT - as well as Google Scholar© (**http://scholar.google.com**).

Both Turn It In and My Drop Box are capable of scanning electronic documents submitted through WebCT and other post-secondary educational services and finding phrases, lines, blocks of text, and even entire term papers or essays that have been published or written by other authors.

Google Scholar© and other general search engines search for strings of text as typed in by the user and are very good at finding plagiarized or sources which have not been properly referenced.

My Instructor or TA Won't Know... Will They?

The easiest answer to that question is, "Of course we will!" There are other means of determining whether or not a student has used work written by another author or student besides search engines and web tools. The easiest one used by instructors is the "use it in a sentence" method.

Instructors spend enough time interacting and talking with their students that they can look at terms or phrases in a paper and ask him or herself, "Does that look right?"

They then approach the student and offers him or her the opportunity to admit the wrongdoing with possibly a reduced sanction for a first-time offence.

If the student insists it is his or her own work, often the instructor will ask the student to use the questionable word or phrase in a sentence - not the sentence in the paper, of course! - in order to determine whether or not the student understands the term completely. If the student cannot do so, it provides further grounds for the instructor to research the assignment or request the student to provide his or her research notes or rough draft to disprove the suspicions of academic dishonesty.

But what if you - or "the friend of your friend" - paid an online service to write an original term paper or assignment guaranteed to pass Turn It In, My Drop Box, and other plagiarism-detection tools? Chances are, since we are bringing it up in this chapter, we have already found most of those websites, and so has your instructor, and you may be required again to provide your research notes or rough draft.

Academic dishonesty is not just about cheating and getting a decent grade for no work. Academic dishonesty unfairly skews the academic records of the cheater, the class, the department, the institution, and ultimately the records of university students as a whole. It is unfair to both the perpetrator and to the rest of the students, because it falsely raises standards and requirements of other students, and the perpetrator learns nothing. If anything, it serves to encourage the perpetrator to do it again in order to maintain the grade point average that was falsely earned in the first place.

Getting caught can mean serious sanctions against the perpetrator, anywhere from a failing grade in the course and having to repeat it, having a blemish on one's academic record which will follow you on your transcripts for the rest of your life, to academic probation or even expulsion from your institution. It is not worth the anxiety over getting caught, the possible guilt if you actually get away with it, or the consequences that follow when you **do** get caught. Our advice: just don't do it.

Enjoy your classes, absorb as much as you can about your subject matter, and make a serious effort at everything. You will not only learn more, but you will become a better, more rounded student and will have more experience to offer in the future, no matter what your endeavour.

Conclusion

Now you have designed a creation that will give you a sense that you have truly created something to be proud of - a document that hangs together logically, represents your honest opinions and thoughts, makes impact, and creates a new level of self-respect so that both you and others respect your ability to think and write more clearly.

Hansen, Randall S., and Hansen, Katherine. (n.d.). What Do Employers Really Want? Top Skills and Values Employers Seek from Job-Seekers. *Quintessential Careers.* Accessed on July 3, 2006 at **www.quintcareers.com/job_skills_values.html**.

It's Just Lunch. (2006). Accessed on July 3, 2006 at **www.itsjustlunch.com**.

Ohio State University (2005). Research and Internet Guides and Tools. *University Libraries.* Accessed on July 3, 2006 at **www.lib.ohio-state.edu/sites/guides/**.

Ibid. (2005). Turabian Citation Guide. *University Libraries.* Accessed on July 3, 2006 at **www.lib.ohio-state.edu/sites/guides/turabiangd.html**.

Purdue University. (2004). Footnotes/endnotes. *Online Writing Lab.* Accessed on July 3, 2006 at **http://owl.english.purdue.edu/workshops/hypertext/apa/parts/footend.html**.

RefWorks. (2006). Accessed on July 3, 2006 at **www.refworks.com**.

The University of Chicago Press. (2006). Turabian, Kate L.: *A Manual for Writers of Term Papers, Theses, and Dissertations.* Accessed on July 3, 2006 at **www.press.uchicago.edu/cgi-bin/hfs.cgi/00/12917.ctl**.

Chapter Four

Understanding the Job of Being a Student

Good judgment comes from experience, and a lot of that comes from bad judgment.
WILL ROGERS

The Job Description

Before you can do a job, you must understand it. Most students who attend university or college don't think of going to school as an important job. They don't even learn about it in high school. But it's like building the foundation of your house. Without a solid foundation, the house will not stand. Without a clear understanding of what the job of "student" requires, it is impossible to do a good job of it.

College or university is often viewed as something that has to be put up with so one can get on with one's life. Some entering students have a "high school" mentality: "If

I have to go to school, I want to do as little work as possible, finish in the least amount of time, get out of there and get a job." But education can be the most important opportunity you will have for building the rest of your life.

Most students aren't aware that many of the people in their lives (instructors, prospective employers, parents and friends) are quite concerned about the quality of their work. Even though it is so important, most students don't really know what the job description for the job of "student" looks like. In fact, many student success and career preparation instructors don't have a student job description, either. Yet, they are expecting and hoping that their students will do the job well! Most students have never seen a job description of any kind. But when you graduate and go to work, the first thing you will get, even before you are hired, is a job description to make sure that you understand the demands and the prerequisites for success of the job. So, we thought it would be very useful for you to see a carefully thought-out job description for the job of student.

A good job description describes the knowledge, skills and abilities needed to effectively perform the clearly-described tasks that are a part of getting the job done well. We have developed the job description for an entering student at most colleges and universities. The requirements are very similar at most institutions.

Job Description of a Student

General Description

The job of "student" is complex and requires a wide range of thinking, writing, speaking, organizational, research and self-management skills. The first-year university student must have completed high school or its equivalent in most cases, although increasingly, post secondary schools no longer require the completion of a high school diploma, although they do have other specific entrance requirements. Successful students will have had some previous success in high school English, science, math, social studies and other courses, or must have completed college preparation courses. Successful full-time students must be able to organize their personal, family, social and economic lives around the requirements of the job.

Knowledge

To be successful in most courses and programs, students must have the following areas of knowledge as prerequisites:

1. Grammar; spelling; correct sentence, paragraph and document structure and organization; punctuation; proof reading; and editing. This knowledge area is critical for success in many writing projects.

2. Mathematics, including a minimum level of algebra for science, statistics for research courses.
3. Library research, including location and extraction of various sources of information for use in writing papers and completing projects and literature reviews.
4. Computer software skills such as word processing, spreadsheets and data bases.
5. Self-knowledge, career and life planning.

Skills

The following skills are necessary to succeed in most college courses and programs:

1. Writing academic papers, research papers, literature reviews;
2. Reading and extracting information from texts and library sources;
3. Taking exams, preparing and reviewing for multiple-choice, essay and short answer exams;
4. Time managing for organizing and planning projects, studying for exams and other assignments;
5. Stress managing to learn to relax, and to prevent stress accumulation and burnout. This is particularly useful around midterm and final exam time; and
6. Critical thinking and writing.

Abilities

The following abilities have to be present or can be developed to better succeed at college or university:

1. Balance of personal, social, work and academic life;
2. Creativity and originality of thought;
3. Consistent follow through on exam preparations, projects and papers;
4. Continuous improvement of the quality of written work through editing and revisions;
5. Successful test taking for academic and job related tests; and
6. Versatility of learning styles to adjust to various types of instructors and professors.

Job Style Requirements

Nearly everyone has seen the conscientious, meticulous student who gets work handed in on time, neatly and correctly presented. Those of us who struggle to perform well at similar academic tasks may, somewhat resentfully, refer to these folks as "nerds." This issue of job style versus personal learning style is perhaps, except for your inborn abilities, the most important factor that can affect your performance as a student. In fact, it can be the greatest block to your success if you don't understand it. However, the good news is that once you understand the work behavioural style requirements of the job better, you can decide to flex your style to meet the demands of the job.

The work behavioural style requirements of the job of "student" are complex and require a great deal of versatility. This fact causes a lot of stress for people adjusting to the pressures of the job of "student." The work behavioural style is a description of the demands of how the job should get done. The basic style tendencies and requirements are listed in order of importance below.

Work Style Tendencies

1. **Action**: drive, result orientation and strategy, extroverted (acts on the physical environment), "left brain" task oriented, linear learning (action oriented occupations such as architect, mechanic, police officer).

2. **Analysis:** sequential, memorization, correctness, attention to details, introverted (accommodates to the environment), "left brain" task-oriented activities, linear learning (analytical occupations such as mathematician, scientist, computer programmer).

3. **Harmonious:** "sit ability," steady working, social learning, balance between right and left brain, and somewhat introverted (accommodates to the social environment) but relationship oriented (service oriented occupations such as teacher, social worker, counselor).

4. **Expressive:** creativity, dramatics, dynamism, originality, "right brain," extroverted (acts upon the social environment) relationship-oriented (entertainment-oriented occupations such as dramatist, musician, artist, communicator).

The job of a student is so complex that it requires a combination of all four style tendencies, but in a certain priority. Analysis is the primary activity of a student; action-orientation to get assignments done on time is secondary; harmony seeking (interpersonal and steadiness) third, and expressiveness, fourth. We have analyzed the work behavioral style requirements of the job of the student using the *Job Style Indicator.*

The kind of a person you are (your predisposition or temperament) is the foundation of your personal style. Your personal style is the foundation of your social and learning style. Your learning style will determine how you approach the job of being a student. If your personal style differs from this job style in any significant way, you will have difficulty flexing into the job.

The most typical difficulty some people have is when they tend not to favour the analytical style. They can have difficulty memorizing, can be less organized and pay less attention to details and quality issues. The second most typical difficulty people have is that they can be less result or action oriented, put off completing assignments, projects and papers, or fail to design a strategy to make sure that they are going to succeed.

You can see how your personal style can influence the results you can get, especially in a negative way, when your personal learning style doesn't match the job style. In the next chapter we will review your personal style and examine how it impacts your performance on the job of being a student.

If you want to complete a Personal Style Indicator you can do one on line at: **http://www.crgleader.com/store/psi-online-access-codes-singles.html**

Others Will Judge You by Your Performance

One of us got a phone call from a student who was discouraged because he had just lost a competition for a policing job to one of his best friends. They were both strong candidates, did well in the interview and finished all the required application requirements. A conversation with the personnel people at the police agency revealed that they had wished that they could have hired them both, but only one position was open. When asked what the decisive factor that made them favor one applicant over the other was, they said that the only thing that wasn't equal was their grades. The person they hired had a grade point average of 3.55 (an "A") and the one they did not hire had a grade point average of 2.93 (a "B").

Eventually, both candidates will have jobs because they are both strong candidates. However, if you were in the position to make the same decision, which candidate would you choose; the one with the 3.55 grade point average or the one with the 2.93? Why would you have made your selection?

Your Grade Report Follows You after Graduation

Your grades from high school rarely follow you around after you graduate from college or university. Most people believe that if you did average in college or university, it doesn't really matter how well you did in high school. How well you do the job of being a university or college student, however, can be a reflection of how well you might do any job. If you are careful, thorough, creative, reliable, conscientious, hard working, resourceful, and can manage, organize and report information well, your instructors or professors are more likely to give you a positive reference when you or your prospective employers ask them to do so. If you barely pass college, people will wonder if you will barely pass if they hire you.

Why Aren't More Students Fired From the Job?

There has been an attitude among instructors, professors and program heads that students are in the midst of a maturation process. Thus, they tend to be somewhat merciful in their approach to evaluating students. At least a few of them tend to be flexible and allow students to turn in assignments late, change the topics of assignments to make them more relevant, and allow students to get to know them at a more personal level. However, as competition heats up and crowding increases, these practices will not occur so frequently. There is a trend to become less tolerant of "slackers," procrastinators, and other people who are generally not ready or willing to take responsibility for producing quality work on time.

Blocks to Doing the Job Well

Rate the extent to which you see yourself as having this difficulty. Insert a number from 1 to 5 in each of the spaces provided below. When you have finished reviewing these common developmental areas, you can add your total score and determine how this book will help you.

5	4	3	2	1
A Great Deal	A Fair Amount	Somewhat	Slightly	Not At All

Success Block A: Negative Attitudes

1._____ **I Have a Negative Attitude That Creates a Low Motivation Level.** Some people have had some painful, negative experiences in their elementary and high school years which may make them believe that all schooling is negative. They are anxious and they don't anticipate that they will do very well. Their attitude is so negative that they really do not try to succeed - because if they did, and failed, their humiliation would be so excruciating that they believe they wouldn't be able to bear it. We have seen this terrible fear amongst underachievers, people who speak English as their second language, people with learning difficulties, and those who, because of their early childhood deprivation, have had difficulty in adjusting to the complexity of school life in their early years.

2._____ **I Have a Naïve "High School" Mentality about Success**. About 1/3 of people who graduated from high school did above average. You may be among this group of people. These same people tend to believe that they will do "just fine" in college or university. While previous grades in high school are the best indicator of future grades, this is not true for over half of those who attend college or university. On average, if you got "B's" in high school, you will have to try to get "C's" in college. If you got "A's," you will have to work hard to get "B's," and so on down the scale. We put the emphasis on "WORK HARD" because most students in high school, particularly in North America, do not work hard. The naïve, high school mentality, when asked to consider the benefits of hard work says, "Uh, right, whatever's cool..." And then proceeds to "party on, dude."

3._____ **I Have A Party Animal Mentality.** The party animal believes that things will work out fine if the need to have fun is taken care of first. Fraternities and sororities teach their initiates well. "If the urge to party creeps up on you then 'get it on' right away so you can alleviate any tension before it mounts any further. After all, the world is in such rough shape we should all just 'eat, drink and be merry, for tomorrow we may die!'" This extreme orientation toward life produces predictable burnout and dropout for many students. Even so, surveys show that the binge-and-purge philosophy of university drinking (and drug use) is on the rise throughout North America. Each year, more and more deaths, accidents and alcohol-related illness are being reported from university campuses.

4._____ **I Lack Resourcefulness.** The attitude of "I just want to get by," and "It's good enough, why should I try and kill myself doing a super job - it doesn't make any real difference anyhow," kills the resourcefulness that could make the difference between a pass and a fail in a course or program. Some students aren't awake when it comes to taking advantage of existing resources like low interest student loans, bursaries, scholarships, personal and academic counselling, part time jobs, and full time summer employment. We can predict with surprising accuracy who will be working in good summer jobs after their first year at university, and who will come around to us in June and ask us if we know where there are any jobs. The same people who dug deep into the library for unique and interesting resources for their papers are the same ones who dug up interesting, well paying, career-related jobs!

5.______ **I Lack "Staying Power."** Commitment and determination are required in order to have staying power. Some people just give up if things don't "feel comfy" for them. They would rather quit school and get a job that pays eight or nine dollars an hour for five or ten years, rather than go to college for a few years, triple their income and do more interesting and challenging work. Because they won't endure some hardships, they get stuck in their restricted lives by lack of opportunity and mobility. Without staying power, either on a part or full time basis, no one completes college and university programs.

6.______ **I am Afraid To Ask Questions.** Some people allow their insecurities and self-doubts to get in the way of asking the questions that are on their minds. They are short-circuiting their learning when they do this. This difficulty, when overcome, will result in accelerated learning, developed relationships with faculty and students, enhanced self-esteem, self-satisfaction and enjoyment of learning.

7.______ **I Lack Self-Knowledge.** Some people are not motivated because they struggle to gain clarity about what to do with their lives and their careers, and why. There appear to be five levels of clarity at which you can live and work.

Now add the numbers. What does the total tell you? Are you on your way to success already, or do you need help, practical advice to succeed in school? Please see the end of this section for a self-reporting analysis.

Success Block B: Lack of Inner Resources

Rate the extent to which you see yourself as having this difficulty.

5	4	3	2	1
A Great Deal	A Fair Amount	Somewhat	Slightly	Not At All

1. **Survival.** Just get any job and hang on to it for money.
2. **Interest.** Get a job I am interested in and hang on to it for money.
3. **Satisfaction.** Get a job I enjoy and hang on to it for self-fulfillment and money.

4. **Service.** Fulfill some needed service I enjoy and receive career satisfaction and self-fulfillment.

5. **Purpose.** Be purpose - (mission) driven, based on clear vision, and enough money and fulfillment come along with them.

If you are living and working at levels 1, 2, or 3, then work is mainly something you do for yourself. You get no sense of satisfaction from making a contribution to anyone else. As you progress through to level 3, there comes a time when you want to make a positive difference in the world around you. This seems to be rather universal for people to be striving for higher levels of actualization (as Abraham Maslow called them).

You May Lack Clarity about Life's Big Issues

If you want to build strong interior structures for your life and career, you will eventually need to clarify and develop the internal areas of health, beliefs, identity, vision, mission, purpose, values, ethics, goals, and the plan and steps for success. These issues are not dealt with quickly by reading one book or taking one course, but we want to list them to assist you to set some longer term personal development goals that could result in your being much more clear about who you really are and where you really want to go. The following is a summary of the internal structures of your life that are a part of your building a personal foundation.

1. **Beliefs Are My Assumptions About:**
   - WHAT is going on here.
   - What is true, real, false, unreal, good and bad.
   - What is the origin, source and purpose of life.
   - What is at the foundation of your life.
   - How should life and love be conducted.
2. **Clearly Understanding Your Identity Is Based On:**
   - WHO and WHAT you believe you are.
   - Experiences with family.
   - Experiences with social groups and school.
   - Success and failure experiences.
   - A vision of what could be possible.
   - A clarification process.

2. Vision is What YOU Believe To Be Possible:

- WHEN dreams are realized.
- For an ennobling future.
- For the future you prefer.
- To inspire and motivate self and others.
- Regarding dreams that could come true.

4. Purpose (or Mission) Is a Public Statement:

- Of WHY you intend to accomplish your vision.
- Of what you intend to accomplish.
- That sets you on fire.
- That can be life long.
- That emerges from a deep and clear sense of vision.

5. Values Are Personal Priorities about What's Important:

- To determine HOW you go about doing things.
- To determine how you treat people.
- To determine your real priorities.
- To determine how you spend your time.

6. Ethics Are Formal Codes of Conduct:

- That are based on values.
- That are agreed upon between parties.
- That are shared by an association of people.
- That can be broken.
- That when broken, can carry penalties.

7. Goals: Should be set after the above are specified.

- Act as well defined targets for accomplishment.
- Are bound by timelines.
- Can include personal, career, team or corporate.
- Are realistic and achievable.
- Are committed to wholeheartedly.

8. Action Plans

- Define steps to achieve goals
- Are behaviorally defined
- Are measurable
- Are bound by timelines
- Are accountable to someone for follow-through

Success Block C: Lack of Academic Skills

Information Handling Skills

Using the same five point rating scale, rate the extent to which you need to develop the skills outlined below.

5	4	3	2	1
A Great Deal	A Fair Amount	Somewhat	Slightly	Not At All

___ I need to develop reading skills.

___ I need to develop memorization skills.

___ I need to develop exam preparation skills.

___ I need to develop library research skills.

___ I need to develop writing skills. I need to develop note taking and debriefing skills.

Success Block D: Lack of Life Skills

Using the same five point rating scale, rate the extent to which you need to develop the skills outlined below.

5	4	3	2	1
A Great Deal	A Fair Amount	Somewhat	Slightly	Not At All

___ I need to develop time management skills.

___ I need to develop stress management skills.

___ I need to develop money management skills.

___ I need to develop verbal articulation and discussion skills.

___ I need to develop organization skills to organize my personal life and the things in it.

Success Block E: Difficult Life Circumstances

Using the same five point rating scale, rate the extent to which you have the needs outlined below.

5	4	3	2	1
A GREAT DEAL	A FAIR AMOUNT	SOMEWHAT	SLIGHTLY	NOT AT ALL

___ I lack money.

___ My family does not give me moral support.

___ My friends are distractions rather than supports.

___ I have a personal crisis.

Summarizing Your Obstacles and Developing an Action Plan

Now that you have had an opportunity to identify what might be in your way of achieving your optimum success, summarize what you have learned from the above 3 assessments and develop an action plan to address those attitudes, issues or skill deficiencies that you need to enhance.

Negative Attitudes	**Attitudes**	**Action Plan**
Life Issues that I Need to Clarify	**Issues**	**Action Plan**
Academic Skills I need to Develop	**Skills**	**Action Plan**

Anderson, T. D., with Robinson, E.T. (1989). *The Job Style Indicator.* Consulting Resource Group International, Inc.: Abbotsford, B.C. Canada.

Chapter Five

Understanding and Developing Yourself as a Learner

If the only tool you have is a hammer, then you tend to go around treating everything as if it were a nail.
ABRAHAM MASLOW

Introduction

Educators seem to have believed for centuries that all they had was a hammer. The depersonalizing effect of a cognitive, linear, rote learning approach has turned many students off from the joys of learning. Educators have primarily been preoccupied, and perhaps even over-obsessed, with cognitive learning and development (analysis of ideas, mathematics, memorization and recall). But there is far more. Maybe they have to substitute the learning of the '3R's" for the development of the whole learner.

You have reviewed the job style requirements for the job of student in the previous chapter. Now we will explore the way you prefer to learn; your *Personal Learning Style*, the understanding of which is important to capitalize on your preferences and strengths and match them with the job demands. Your personal learning style will help you to maximize your strengths and develop your weaker areas.

For further learning success, *Integrative Learning* will be introduced toward the second half of this chapter so that you can understand and develop your multiple intelligences. *Integrative Learning* is an innovative philosophy of learning that is changing how education is delivered throughout all levels in the school system. In this chapter we will examine the extent to which you have developed your seven intelligences and explore ways for you to further develop them.

Your Personal Learning Style and Success

You have probably begun to get a sense that your personal style may not perfectly match the requirements of the job of being a student, but you aren't sure how. To approximate what your style is, you can take several steps. We recommend that you implement all three steps to take advantage of learning this area of self knowledge that affects everything you do.

Option One. Use the *Quick Personal Learning Style Assessment* at **http://www.engr.ncsu.edu/learningstyles/ilsweb.html**. This will get you started and provide you with a "ballpark" approximation of your personal style preferences. You will then see how these compare with the job style requirements. This quick version combines some of the dimensions included in personal style and learning style assessment. It is not an accurate psychometric test, but can give you a good start in understanding and flexing your style. This can improve your grades.

Option Two. Order a copy of the *Personal Style Indicator (PSI)* which will provide you with a comprehensive self-assessment of your personal style, believed to be the foundation of your learning style. This assessment costs about $25.00 and can be found at **www.crgleader.com**. Ordering information can be found at the back of this chapter. The PSI is the lowest cost self-assessment tool of its kind and provides you with an in-depth interpretation of your:

- General tendencies;
- Strengths,
- Areas of difficulty,
- Style of managing stress,

- Style of functioning on a team, and
- Style of leading and following.

It will also give you specific recommendations for improving your performance.

Option Three. Order the *PSI for Learners (PSI-L)* and gain insight into the factors that are specifically learning style related. This assessment is also available at **www.crgleader.com**.

As you look at your scores, you should be able to see where your personal learning style preferences don't match the requirements of the job graph. You can learn to "pump" your *analysis* up, get your *expressiveness* down, inflate or decrease your *harmonious* tendencies or become more action oriented. This can increase your effectiveness and your grades.

The impact of your personal style on your approach to learning is profound. You can get turned on or off by the learning environment you are in.

The idea behind understanding your style is to capitalize on the strengths of your style and compensate for or develop areas where you have weaknesses.

Your Learning Style and Your Instructor's Teaching Style May Not Mesh

Some of your instructors may teach in the style opposite to your learning preference. This can cause some problems for you, especially if you haven't developed much versatility in how to approach different teachers. When this occurs, there are several things you can do to remedy the problem.

- Change classes so you can get into another instructor's class (this is the "chicken's" way out because you won't develop the capacity to adapt to various teaching styles).
- Develop in your weaker and less preferred areas so your learning style more closely approaches the instructor's teaching style (in the long run this will increase your grade point average more than the previous approach). It can also prepare you to work with a variety of individual styles in your chosen profession.
- Communicate with your instructor and negotiate ways to make the course more interesting and relevant to you (this can be very helpful, especially when you have a flexible instructor).

Your Seven Intelligences

Since the mid-1980s, *Integrative Learning* has become increasingly implemented as a learner-centred approach to delivering any curriculum all over North America. For the learner as well as the educator, one of the great breakthroughs of this relatively new approach is the evidence that there are multiple intelligence capabilities within each person and that to some extent all seven of them should be developed if the learning environment is designed properly.

You will likely begin to get excited, as we did, when you look at these intelligences for yourself. They are outlined below in summary form. As you read them, insert a number from 1-5 that represents your estimate of your current ability beside each intelligence area.

5	4	3	2	1
A Great Deal	A Fair Amount	Somewhat	Slightly	Not At All

Rating Your Seven Intelligences

Linguistic Intelligence: Having sensitivity to language, meanings, and the relations among words. Typically found in: novelists, poets, copywriters, scriptwriters, editors, magazine writers, reporters, public relations directors and speech writers.

Your estimate:_____

Musical Intelligence: Having sensitivity to pitch, rhythm, timbre and the emotional power and complex organization of music. Typically found in: performers, composers, conductors, musical audiences, recording engineers and those who build musical instruments.

Your estimate:_____

Logical-Mathematical Intelligence: Engaging in abstract thought, precision, counting, organization, and logical structure. Typically found in: mathematicians, scientists, engineers, animal trackers, police investigators and lawyers.

Your estimate:_____

Spatial Intelligence: Possessing keen observation, visual thinking, mental images, metaphor and a sense of the whole gestalt (picture). Typically found in: architects, painters, sculptors, navigators, chess players, naturalists, theoretical physicists and battlefield commanders.

Your estimate:_____

Bodily-Kinesthetic Intelligence: Exercising control of one's body and of objects, having good timing and trained responses that function like reflexes. Typically found in: dancers, athletes, actors, inventors, mimes, surgeons, karate teachers and the mechanically gifted.

Your estimate:_____

Interpersonal Intelligence: Having sensitivity to others and an ability to read the intentions and desires of others and potentially to influence them. Typically found in: politicians, teachers, religious leaders, counselors, salespeople and leaders.

Your estimate:_____

Intrapersonal Intelligence: Possessing self-knowledge, sensitivity to one's own values, purpose, feelings, a developed sense of self. Typically found in: novelists, counselors, wise elders, philosophers and people with a deeper sense of self.

Your estimate:_____

Now review your estimates. Our guess is that you will find that you are strong in some if not all of these intelligences. Which is your stronger intelligence? Which is your weakest? In the following pages, we will discuss the significance of these intelligences and some suggestions to develop them.

We would also like to highlight one related topic, Emotional Intelligence (EQ). We highly recommend a particular research in this area by Debra Vandervoort that suggests that developing these intelligences can not only be one of your winning cards in university, it can dramatically change your success in life generally (see the end of this chapter).

The theory of multiple intelligences could be the beginning of a revolution in the way we understand and develop human potential from pre-school through adulthood. Curriculum designers, educators and parents are all rethinking what people should be learning, how they should learn, and how teaching must be radically transformed in order to address the development of the whole person. By understanding and applying the knowledge in this chapter, you can design a whole new way of thinking about yourself as a learner that can revolutionize how you grow as a person and succeed as a student.

If we were designing a whole new educational system, we certainly wouldn't want to omit any one of the seven intelligences, would we? That is exactly what many teachers do now. Which two intelligences receive over 80 percent of the emphasis in what is currently thought of as mainstream, valid, important education? The linguistic and logical-mathematical! Yet, it is the other intelligences that determine much of our true success and satisfaction in our daily lives!

Why are the two "L's" given such elite status and emphasized so much in college and university? The full reasons are likely complex, but primarily involve the fact that the Age of Reason has moved us through the Industrial Age into the Information-Service Age. To be analytical, reasonable, clear-thinking and knowledgeable, has meant, and still means, power, control and money! It is technology spurred by intellectual and research breakthroughs (and their power advantages) that won World War II and perhaps has forestalled World War III so far. It is the analytical mind that discovered and refined the vaccine for polio and is slowly but surely closing in on one for AIDS. No wonder people value these two intelligences so much.

We don't mean to say that the two "L's" should be given less importance or emphasis than they are currently given. But the problem with the present imbalance in emphasis is that our educational systems now label students with lower potential or development in these two areas as "below average" students (implying they are below average people) by not counting them as "academic" in nature when they take courses such as music, drama, art, creative writing, journalism, and mechanics). It is no wonder those people whose primary tendency is not in the two "L" areas say that they don't like school!

In fact, the job analysed as being the most complex of all is that of the mechanic who must understand the theories and applications of electronics, physics, mechanics, hydraulics and pneumatics. But mechanics do not enjoy the same status and earnings as, for example, lawyers, who often make double or triple the mechanic's salary. This is in spite of the fact that about the same amount of time is required to study to become a certified mechanic as to become a lawyer.

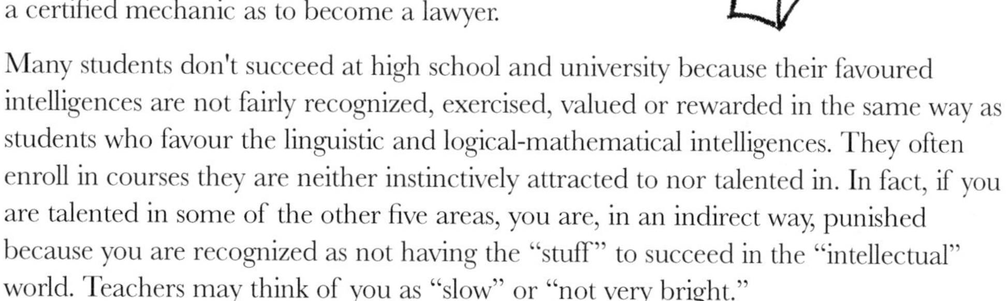

Many students don't succeed at high school and university because their favoured intelligences are not fairly recognized, exercised, valued or rewarded in the same way as students who favour the linguistic and logical-mathematical intelligences. They often enroll in courses they are neither instinctively attracted to nor talented in. In fact, if you are talented in some of the other five areas, you are, in an indirect way, punished because you are recognized as not having the "stuff" to succeed in the "intellectual" world. Teachers may think of you as "slow" or "not very bright."

On the other hand, people who are talented in the two "L's" are often called "nerds" by those who aren't. Many cerebrally-oriented doctors, for example, make terrible surgeons and their bedside manner is atrocious. And of course, there is the stereotype of the inwardly-preoccupied, "absent-minded" professor who is unaware of, and uninvolved in, life around him.

For some years to come, you will continue to see a heavy emphasis on the two "L's," because administrators and teachers won't quickly change how they do things. They aren't likely to enroll in a comprehensive new training program on how to teach the development of multiple intelligences, and may not even believe in such a thing. Previous research, reported by Martel and Kline, emphasizes that the applications of integrative learning have evidenced striking successes.

- The Simon Guggenheim Elementary School in Chicago reports an increase of 103% in the number of students completing reading and math requirements as a direct result of implementing Integrative Learning.
- After a two year implementation of Integrative Learning technologies, students in the Paradise, California school district gamed 1.5 times the learning accomplishment compared to control groups, as measured by the California Achievement Tests.
- At Prince George's Community College, the Federal Health and Human Services Agency has awarded a grant to completely redesign the Nursing Curriculum on the principles of Integrative Learning. Over 50 faculty members have been trained with Integrative Learning technologies over a period of two years. Students enhanced their performance compared with students who were trained with traditional methods. In addition to improved performance, dropout rates dropped drastically compared to the normal 40 to 50% dropout rate of control groups.

There are many other encouraging studies, but what does this mean to you? What can you do to develop enough versatility and ingenuity to make sure that if you struggle at all with the two "L's", that you gain skill in these, and other areas? We can offer you the good news that you can learn to apply some of the integrative learning technologies to your learning processes whether your instructor or professor knows what you are doing or not. This will help you not only pass but excel in college.

Make the Internal Paradigm Shift to Becoming a Lean Mean Learning Machine

A paradigm is a way of assuming that things must be, or how they must be done. For example, until 1966, the Swiss cornered over 80% of the world's market on watches. They were the master watch makers of the world. At a conference, one of their more innovative watch makers introduced the electronic quartz crystal movement that nearly eliminated the need for precision in the complex and delicate mechanical movements. They scorned him and laughed him out of the conference for coming up with such a preposterous idea! However, there was one Japanese visitor to that same conference who quite liked the idea and developed a version of it himself in Japan. His name was Mr. Seiko. You know the rest of the story. Now, the Swiss are struggling to hang onto 30% of the world's market for watches, and the Japanese dominate. The same thing happened in the quality movements with vehicles in Japan. The United States has been shamed into producing higher quality automobiles at a globally competitive price! Both the Swiss and the Americans have had to make a **paradigm shift** to a new way of doing things. So do you!

Once you know yourself as a learner and understand your more and less preferred intelligences, you can set out a plan for your development as a learner. This plan will help you identify the areas you need to "beef up" to avoid failure or lower grades than you are capable of.

To better understand yourself as a learner and make the shift to learning more effectively using all your learning "equipment," you have to break out of your old ruts. Here is a list of things that you could do to consider making the paradigm shift from your old way of learning to the new integrative way. Check the integrative learning ideas you want to implement.

See the chart below to learn more about the differences between "old paradigm" learning and integrative learning.

Old Paradigm	**Integrative Learning Paradigm**
Read for hours: your mind wanders	Read in 20-30 minute shots with brief breaks
Take long notes while reading	Make 3 X 5 note cards of main points
Study while dance music is playing	Study with music that helps you focus
Study alone when it doesn't work	Study in small groups: talk about key points
Sit at the back of class	Sit toward the front of class, interact with professor
Talk with others during lecture	Debrief with others after lecture
Take long pages of lecture notes	Make short notes on 3 X 5 note cards
Try to imagine what will be on tests	Inquire from others what will be tested
Review your notes before exams	Review 3 X 5 cards three times per week before exams

Study in silence	Study with music that helps you focus
Study while dance music is playing	Study with music that helps you focus
Stay in the class of every instructor	Switch classes to instructors you learn from
Do whatever assignments you are told	Negotiate for more interesting assignments
When memorizing, review three times	When memorizing, review each piece of information seven times
Become what your parents want you to	Decide your own career goals and go for them
Spend a lot of time partying	Party to celebrate successes
Watch TV for 2-3 hours a day	Watch videos that are course related 2 hours per week
Rent videos and watch movies	Make videos as presentations for classes
Play computer games	Use computers as tools to ace courses
Dread tests like the black plague	Enjoy the feeling of preparing for and acing tests
Study on your bed, have friends over	Set up an office where you have control and privacy
Watch more TV	Exercise while reviewing flash cards
Continue to accept vague goals	Set tentative career goals based on interests and abilities
Study alone more	Set up a study group of other motivated students
Remain vague about what your purpose is	Actively search for clarity of personal purpose
Worry a lot about exams	Test yourself until you know what you know. Use flash cards
You never know what will be on exams	Anticipate and target for exam items while studying

Capitalizing On Your Seven Intelligences to Improve Your Grades

We are going to review the seven intelligences again. This time, you will get even more specific ideas about how you can beef up your inborn capabilities.

1. Linguistic Intelligence

Linguistic Intelligence: Having sensitivity to language, meanings, and the relations among words. Typically found in: novelists, poets, copywriters, scriptwriters, editors, magazine writers, reporters, public relations directors, and speech writers.

You are fortunate if you tend to prefer Linguistic Learning activities, because the careful selection of words and weaving of meanings is central to success at college. If you don't prefer this area or just haven't ever tried to develop it, you may be surprised at how much you can excel

74

with some focused effort and the right assistance. This is truly something you will need to work on as a high priority, even if it is an area of strength from high school or previous employment. Writing standards are high and you want to do well at school and in your job after school. People will judge your professionalism by how well you can write! There are some specific things anyone can do to develop this intelligence:

- **Don't put off learning to write!** Decide to become a writer. If this has been a problem area for you and you put off learning how to do it well, your grades will surely suffer significantly! If you get on it from the beginning and decide to learn to write, you will gain ground.
- **Get a tutor** and learn writing skills because you want to do so for your own success (perhaps for the first time).
- **Use a proof reader** who knows the English language to proof and edit all your written assignments before you hand them in to your instructor.
- **Read other students' papers!** You will be amazed at the range of quality you will see. Then you will be able to see how well you write compared to others. This will put you in the instructor's chair and you will then see more clearly why you tend to get the grades you get!
- **Ask your professor to read the rough draft of your paper** before you are required to hand in the final draft. Some will do this, others will not. Make sure you have done most of the work and it is your best shot. Don't expect your instructor to be your editor, proof reader and tutor. Most of them simply don't have the time to do all that! However, it is always to your advantage to get feedback in advance whenever possible. Then, make the necessary changes and impress your professor with your initiative. Simply ask the professor, "Is it your practice to do a brief pre-read of a rough draft of a paper so I can get some general feedback?"
- **Use a modern word processor** on a computer. If you can't afford to purchase one, most colleges and universities have some available for student use if you book time on them. You can also often find free computer training classes that get you up and running in a few hours word processing your documents. The word processor should have a spelling checker, grammar checker, a thesaurus and dictionary built in. Learn to use this incredible tool as early as you can - preferably before you get to university or college. All other professions have tools. This is one that is well worth your investing in - it will improve your grades if you know how to use it!

- **Have other students review your paper**, especially if you know they are good writers. Get agreement from several students to read one another's papers while you eat lunch or have coffee together. This can be a great way to learn. Watch how other writers write. You will be doing a great deal of reading. Take mental note of how they are handling word selection, sentence and paragraph structure, document organization, grammar, spelling, etc. This will help you to be a more conscious reader and more alert writer.

- **Take a course in writing.** Most colleges and universities require you to take introductory English composition. Often instructors in these courses ask you to read some essays or stories, and then write your own essays about them. Unfortunately, they often give precious little direction about how you can write better. In fact, most of these educators are so tired of seeing poor writing and seeing so few students make significant strides, that they are discouraged and offer little specific feedback for improvement. It is such hard work to edit and correct other peoples' work! So don't expect most people in introductory courses to give you much feedback. Use the services of the writing centre at your college or university. Many institutions have recognized the common problem that students have in learning to write well and often set up writing centers. These centers are staffed by paid personnel or volunteer faculty. Quite often, to use this service, you must first create a work to the best of your ability, sign up for an appointment and show up on time. The person assisting you will give you pointers on how to improve your work.

- **Take courses from instructors who emphasize writing** if you are good at it or are willing to improve. This will improve your grades. It is true that some instructors count a larger percentage of your final grade on written assignments than others in the same course. Also, some instructors give written exams where your strengths will be able to shine.

- **Take courses from instructors who emphasize less written work** and more projects or multiple choice exams if you struggle with written work. Again, some instructors simply have different emphases on the amount and kinds of work they assign. You can use this to your advantage by finding out what has been required in the past from previous course outlines (usually in the library or in the Student Services Office). Previous students can also tell you how the individual instructor emphasizes various requirements.

2. Musical Intelligence

Musical Intelligence: Having sensitivity to pitch, rhythm, timbre, and the emotional power and complex organization of music.

Typically found in: performers, composers, conductors, musical audiences, recording engineers and makers of musical instruments.

You may think that this area doesn't have much to do with academic success. However, it can make a significant difference. If you can become involved in courses or programs where these abilities are important, assessed, recognized and rewarded, then your grade point average goes up!

The most obvious advice here is to major or minor in music if you have talent in this area, or want to develop latent intelligence. As adults, some people find that they are far more musically inclined than they had expected because they had few opportunities to become involved as children. These people find that they are positively motivated to learn about music and develop their skills.

- **Use music as a study aid.** There is evidence that certain kinds of music facilitate learning for many people. It can shut out distractions and enable a new level of concentration and focus. For example, a number of high school math teachers suggest that their students use an mp3 player if they are distracted by other students in class while they are doing math work. But use caution! Some music can become a major distraction. The kind of music can differ significantly from person to person, but baroque classical music (such as Bach) being played quietly in the background has been found to be most effective for a number of people. Some people want to rock out on their math. If it works, do it.

- **Use music while reviewing note cards** or for memorizing during repetitive study sessions. Quiet background music can break up the monotony of studying the same information over and again until full recall is attained, and acts as a stimulus for recall in many people. Some people can do rote learning faster with music playing than without it. A few other people find that they must have absolute quiet in order to focus their attention.

- **Use music in your presentations in various classes.** Music can capture attention or sustain it in some people who hear your speeches or presentations in classes. If you design your music for your presentation and your audience, you will likely get a positive response that can affect your overall grade on the presentation.

3. Logical-Mathematical Intelligence

Logical-Mathematical Intelligence: Engaging in abstract thought, precision, counting, organization, or logical structure. Typically found in: mathematicians, scientists, engineers, police investigators and lawyers.

You are fortunate if you have developed this area of your character already, because it is about equal in importance to the linguistic area to your success at college. If this is your strength, you will find that instructors whose presentation is abstract, logical, organized and precise will highly value your papers, exam responses, projects and presentations. Many professors admire the intellectual prowess that is required in order to contrast and compare complex theories. It is even possible that the professor could have a certain amount of academic "pride" in some of those who have the ability well-developed. Some people look down on those who have difficulty with or do not prefer this area of intelligence - they may think of them as "dumb." Only a minority of the population has this ability developed early in life and these children are termed "gifted" or "accelerated." It has only been in recent years that the other intelligences have been recognized as worthy of recognition and special classes.

If you aren't especially developed in this area, or just aren't interested in it, you have a problem to deal with when facing university or college work! To become more capable of thinking clearly, handling ideas logically and with care is perhaps the main traditional goal of university. You must develop this area of your ability to ensure that you will do better in college. Listed below are some ideas that will assist you to develop this area of your intelligence.

Get a logic coach. Find someone who is particularly capable at organizing, explaining and analyzing ideas (whether they are mathematical or philosophical) and spend time learning how this person handles information in books and from lectures. Get them to critique your work in terms of its organization, logic and structure. Rewrite your paper based on their feedback. This person might be your roommate, your spouse, your instructor or professor, or someone in the writing centre. Some universities even have Critical Thinking centres and courses in logic (usually in the philosophy departments) where students learn to do critical thinking.

Use the outlining program in your word processor. If you learn to use an outlining program or at least plan your academic papers using the outline approach, you will have greater success. Get some help at first because if you aren't used to thinking in this manner, it will seem strange to you. Simply put, in designing an outline what you do is plan the content and sequence of your headings and main points under them. For example, the first draft of this book was built upon a logically-organized outline.

For math, get a math tutor. Don't try to go it alone if you have to take a math course or a statistics course, especially if you got "C's" or less in high school math. It will be less expensive in the long run to hire a tutor than to take the course all over again. It is less expensive emotionally as well. It is a humiliating experience for many students to be perceived as "dumb" in mathematics. This area of intelligence develops at different times and rates for various people.

4. Spatial Intelligence

Spatial Intelligence: Keen observation, visual thinking, mental images, metaphor, a sense of the whole gestalt (picture). Typically found in: architects, painters, sculptors, navigators, chess players, naturalists, theoretical physicists and battlefield commanders.

If this area comes naturally for you, it can be a strength because you can use it to build your success. This intelligence is especially important if you are entering those occupations which require such talents (see above). However, you can develop this ability to visualize how to plan your career, your study strategy, or manage your time and money. One professor (Terry Anderson) explains it this way:

For example, this is an area that I found particularly natural. When I entered college I wasn't sure what I wanted to do until I saw a particular person teaching introductory psychology in a particular way. Once I could see the potential for myself doing a similar job I began envisioning it in my own future. I became more motivated, goal-directed, and, for the first time in my life, had a purpose for studying. The vision of my success as a teacher of psychological principles remained clearly in my mind's eye and as a result I have been teaching such courses for over 20 years. I consider myself an "architect" of my own life designs. The consequences have been profound for me and others in my life.

- **Decide that you want to develop this critical area of your intelligence.** It will open up opportunities that you had not considered for your career and your life. In fact, it could be a primary determining factor in the kind and quality of life you live at all levels.

- **Take a course in career and life planning.** Learn to envision end states or alternative scenarios as though you were designing your life and your career from the perspective of looking down from the moon, and you will gain a distinct advantage. Courses that develop such capacities are offered at most colleges and universities and can be taken during the evenings even while you are a junior or senior in high school.

- **See a career and life-planning counselor.** Most colleges and universities have full-time counselors you can see free of charge to do career and life planning. Some high school counselors are also trained to provide such service. You can increase your chances of having a career for your life if you look into this very important area and develop the "big picture" capabilities of your mind.

5. Bodily-Kinesthetic Intelligence

Bodily-Kinesthetic Intelligence: Exercising control of one's body and of objects, timing, trained responses that function like reflexes. Typically found in: dancers, athletes, actors, inventors, mimes, surgeons, karate teachers and the mechanically gifted.

If you have developed this area of bodily intelligence, you are fortunate because, as you live the (somewhat sedentary) student life, you are then more likely to engage in activities that prevent student burnout and the accumulation of fat (resulting in heart disease). Perhaps more than most jobs, the job of student can cause you to feel pain in your neck, shoulders and spine. This can be caused from a number of things, but surely the hours required studying, writing papers, and preparing for exams add up. Many of these hours involve sitting relatively still. Our bodies do not do this healthily for hours on end. If you develop this intelligence, you will be more likely to become involved in athletic activities, practice fitness routines and de-stress the tensions of student life. You can bring into your life those things that act as energizers, stress management activities and fun!

- **Count fitness, sport and activity a high priority!** Sign up for college physical education courses where you will learn to become more adept, more coordinated and have fun playing. The cardiovascular benefits will pay off as the years of student life go by and you won't gain the 15-30 pounds of fat typically gained by non-active students while attending university or college. This is especially important if you are entering an occupation like criminal justice worker (police, corrections, immigration, customs, and security) where physical fitness and coordination are often a requirement of the job itself.

- **Become a member of a gym or fitness centre.** Such centres offer a wide range of fitness activities and exercises, have professional trainers and provide release from pent up stress and strain.
- **Dance your socks off.** Some people enjoy dancing and enjoy it even more when they learn to do it well. You can take lessons and develop movement intelligence, gain health, prevent disease and get better grades as an indirect result.

You may think that this is of little importance compared to the others when it comes performing well at college or university, especially if you have never given exercise and movement much of a priority before. There is research which indicates that those who are enrolled in courses that develop this area of intelligence get better grades.

Sixth is the area of Interpersonal Intelligence

Interpersonal Intelligence: Sensitivity to others, ability to read the intentions and desires of others and potentially to influence them. Typically found in: politicians, teachers, religious leaders, counsellors, salespeople and leaders.

Other than the intrapersonal area, there is perhaps no other area of intelligence that has gone so neglected. Schools often do not attempt to develop this ability directly (except in specialized programs), particularly in high schools and universities. Elementary schools have traditionally made an indirect attempt at "social skills development," but until recently it wasn't even included as an integral part of the curriculum. There is a movement for it to receive the attention that it deserves.

Being socially undeveloped is a big personal disadvantage, and can cause severe stress. This can interfere with intellectual functioning in other areas - being socially unhappy can interfere with academic success. The most common reasons students give for "blowing a semester" are, "broken heart," "problems with my girlfriend or boyfriend," "family problems," or "conflicts at work." In order to develop this area of intelligence, some ideas are outlined below:

- **Take the interpersonal part of your intellectual development seriously.** This area of your mind is so critical to your sense of self-worth (how you feel about yourself inside) and self-esteem (how you think other people see you). It can make or break your career! A social jerk is no fun to work with, doesn't consistently get promoted and is becoming less and less acceptable. Whether you can love or be loved, your success at intimate relationships such as with spouse and children, family, and friends, primarily depend on your developing this area of your self.
- **Take courses or workshops that assist you to develop your social intelligence.** These courses are often titled, *Interpersonal Communications, Human Relations, Managing Conflict, Dealing with Difficult People, Assertiveness Training, Developing Relationships,* and so on. These courses or workshops should not be confused with "communications" courses that are focused on the development of radio and television broadcasting, writing communications or public speaking skills. During the past five to ten years, interpersonal development courses have most often been offered as a part of various programs that prepare you for jobs that require you to deal with people effectively (nursing, medicine, social work, criminal justice work, business). In an age of information and service, these skills and abilities are critical job-keeping skills and help in the achievement of promotions.
- **Seek personal counselling to learn interpersonal skills.** There are many counsellors who work individually and in groups to assist in this area of development. This is perhaps the more powerful and concentrated way to learn these skills and would be appropriate for those who have some history of dysfunction in their personal or family lives.
- **Read about and study the area of interpersonal skills development.** There are a number of books that can help you gain general understanding of social intelligence and how it is developed.

7. Intrapersonal intelligence

Intrapersonal Intelligence: Possessing self-knowledge, sensitivity to one's own values, purpose, feelings, a developed sense of self. Typically found in: novelists, counsellors, wise elders, and philosophers.

This area of intelligence is the most neglected of all. Most people spend more time planning their vacations than they spend developing the internal aspects of their lives. In elementary and high school, there is no focus in the curriculum to develop this intelligence. In college and university there are some opportunities for development, but they are not considered of primary importance. There are some exceptions, but they are few, and where the exceptions do occur, they are considered "peripheral to the core curriculum" - as though one's self is not a central issue that should be considered and developed in a school setting.

Whether you are entering college or university from high school or returning to school after a time of working or raising a family, your time spent at college can be an extraordinary opportunity to develop your intrapersonal intelligence. There are more resources for self-development than most people are aware of. There are books, audio tapes, personal development groups, openly communicative relationships that facilitate learning, courses, workshops, seminars - all of which can be valuable in stimulating the development of this foundational intelligence.

In Conclusion

We want you to graduate from university as a more developed and whole person who has enjoyed success at university and looks forward to the expanding opportunities you have before you to make a good living doing what you love, and have a healthy life with positive relationships that make you happy. Learning how to learn, and becoming a continuous learner is your key to furthering your lifetime success and enjoyment.

Gardner, Howard. 1985. *Frames of Mind: The theory of Multiple Intelligences.* New York: Basic Books.

Vandervoort, Debra J. 2006. *The Importance of Emotional Intelligence in Higher Education.* University of Hawaii, Hilo, USA

Anderson, T.D., Robinson, E.T. (1988, 2000, 2006). *The Personal Style Indicator.* Consulting Resource Group International, Inc. http://www.CRGLeader.com.

Chapter Six

Defining the Challenge and Building the Benefits

The greatest challenge to any thinker is stating the problem in a way that will allow a solution.
BERTRAND RUSSELL

Introduction

After attending school for many years between us, we want to share with you what we have found out about being students, planning our lives, and succeeding, to some extent, at these tasks. Think of us as your best friends who just returned after years away. We are going to tell you some quick facts, with no B.S. We want you to benefit from our unique learning with information that you may not get from friends or parents. In fact, the learning we share with you will likely be different from what your friends and parents might say to you. We will be blunt, to the point, realistic and perhaps funny. You have a lot of work to do and you don't need to spend so much time reading a book about success that it detracts from your success.

Think about your life as a house that you want to build. Let's start with an assessment of the land you want to build on. What kind of land is it? How big is the house going to be? How much work will it take to build it? What will it cost? What will the benefits be of living in this house? As you read the next section we will come back to the analogy of building the house of your life and future.

How to Succeed in the Educational System

Work Hard in Your Job as Student

The one thing that we have had to face from the beginning is that doing a good job of being a college or university student requires a tremendous amount of work. Think about high school. How much time did you spend working on school work outside of class? Possibly not much. But to succeed at college or university, you will have to change all that. This is discouraging to those who like most folks have friends, part-time jobs, and are engaged in some kind of activities such as sports, hobbies, and perhaps even a life on the side!

You may feel that you have some good reasons not to excel at college or university, but there are some facts you should look at first:

- **You may have learned to hate school work.** One of the reasons is that many people are not fully developed intellectually during high school. Then they lost the motivation to work harder, because teachers told them that they didn't measure up, so why try? The good news is that intellectual ability is something that continually gains strength until well into the late 20s and beyond.
- **You may not have been motivated to succeed in school.** Before college, we were on the drop-out or sleep-through-school list. Like most young people in high school, we weren't motivated to succeed because we didn't have a clue about what we wanted. Many students who did mediocre work in high school come back to college and do very well!
- **You may have been struggling through self-worth, family or economic problems.** Many of our friends in high school had problems that interfered with their success in high school. But you can realize your self worth, work out family matters and arrange your romances to embrace success!

- **You may have an action-oriented or social learning style** (rather than an analytical learning style) and instinctively did not want to put up with the typical "dump and scratch" method of education. The dump and scratch approach to teaching can be typical of high school education (the teacher is required to dump the information in the current curriculum in the students, and the students scratch their heads in an effort to find something relevant and useful. Students are often not able to do so and mentally "check out", and barely pass). In college or university, your motivation and ability levels can be dramatically different! Often you will be taking courses that you choose to take because you want to try them out or because you have a serious interest developed in that area.

If you are among those of us who struggled through or dropped out of high school, we have a major word of caution. Don't judge your potential ability or future motivation by how you did in high school! There are too many factors that contribute to success - and most of these factors come on stronger during people's young and mid-adult lives, not necessarily in their teen lives.

Adult education is becoming increasingly oriented toward having students learn theory and principles that have application potential in the real world. Good educators feel a responsibility to insure relevant and meaningful learning. They want to see that it makes people's lives better, their minds enriched, and that society can benefit as an indirect result.

There are, of course, some instructors who still practice the "dump and scratch" method, and you have to learn to deal with their approach as well. This approach has some value in training you to handle large amounts of information quickly and efficiently. We will help you learn to deal with both types of learning situations. The main point is that you can be optimistic about your success because you will bring more maturity, motivation and focus to the task than you did previously, even though there is more than double the work involved at college than at high school. With this in mind, hard work will be something that you will want to do to get your "'house" built so you can live at a higher standard: financially, intellectually, personally, and socially.

Prepare for Rising Standards

Why are good grades important and what can you do about it? There is some hard news. The standards for entering colleges and universities are steadily rising, as are the standards for succeeding. In most areas, there are more students than there are spaces for them. As more people are unemployed in tough economic times, more of them will go back to school and flood the entry gates. And with college budgets shrinking, the competition for entry increases. The institutions of higher learning solve this problem by increasing their admission fees. Some universities admit students on the basis of high school grade point averages, others on SAT (Scholastic Aptitude Tests) or other standardized test scores. Grading standards can also get tougher as instructors' classes bulge - tougher exams reduce class sizes earlier in the semester and even prevent some students from returning the following semester. So what can you do in the face of these kinds of problems?

Don't give up - there is some good news.

If you are having doubts about your ability to compete for entry or success at college, find out about the programs in your area of study that will help you to meet your needs. Inquire at your college or university student services centre.

- If a time commitment is a potential barrier, there are often programs that assist students to begin part time.
- If you have low high school grades, you can take college preparatory courses.
- To help you get your finances in order, student loans are available at low interest rates.
- If you need to finish high school, there is the GED (General Education Development) test for students to attain a high school equivalency certificate - often a prerequisite for entry into colleges and universities

If you can only get into one class that you need, demonstrate that you have the ability to pass even one course with a "C" or better, and things will open up. You can qualify for entry into more courses or programs. You can steadily increase your academic performance by learning how to learn and study while you work part- or full-time.

You Are Not Alone

Everyone is unusually busy at colleges and universities! Instructors are doing research and writing projects, preparing for courses, creating or scoring exams, talking with students, grading papers and quizzes. You may feel like just another student number on the instructor's class list. If you are living away from home, the depersonalizing nature of a college or university environment can cause culture shock, loneliness, even a sense of being de-selfed! This can be especially true during the first semester of your academic life when you don't know many people, you aren't sure you can live up to the required standards, and you may not be sure of your personal identity or direction. This can be a time of feeling like a stranger in a strange land. One 18-year-old, contemplating college, put it this way: "I have size 12 feet, my body is 5'10" tall, and I look like I should still be in high school - I'm not going to college until next year!" A 45-year-old stated, "I don't know ANYONE at the college. I feel so self-conscious and I barely passed high school. I really want to become a teacher, but I sometimes wonder if I am in the wrong place!"

If you know that these feelings are normal, then you can better enjoy all the positive aspects of the new and stimulating learning environment that can give you the feeling that your whole life has just been raised one complete level. One of the authors reports the following experience: "I had the pleasant experience (after I passed all five courses in my first semester with a "C" or better) that I really believed that I could become nearly anything that I wanted to! I never felt that kind of confidence or boldness prior to that first semester's success in college. My first year success (compared to my high school, rock-and-roll, surf life) can be partly attributed to my girlfriend who was academically-oriented, ambitious, and influential enough to woo me into studying before we went out together. I actually enjoyed the time we spent together more when I had first accomplished wiring the house of my future by doing my homework."

Choosing friends carefully can be a great stimulus to success and can break the "stranger" barrier. Getting to know an instructor or a professor after class or during office hours is possible, especially with some, and this can add a great deal of value to your learning experience. Avoid the pitfall some students fall into: turning into a whiner, a critic, or a revolutionary just to make a friend, as insecure people can sometimes do. Instructors and professors are busy, they are people, they have stress, and need recognition and friendship - and so do other students, like you. Being a "suckie" or cool manipulator is very uncool! An open and honest approach to making friends, solving real problems, and meeting real needs works best. You will get respect and earn credibility that way.

Do this assignment! Write 10 pages summarizing the main tenets of Radical Criminology by next class! Get ready for that test on the Crebbs cycle for biology next week. Memorize 60 terms for introductory psychology to prepare for the mid-term.

You often have no choice about what your assignments will be - just like high school again! Not necessarily. Assignments will usually be connected to the objectives of the course you have decided to take, which will make them relevant to you. If they are not relevant, you can often negotiate with your instructor or professor about modifying the topic for a paper or assignment so that what you do suddenly becomes personally interesting! For example, if you are given an assignment to write about "the impact of the Civil War on the North American economy," you may ask to have it changed to "the impact of war on my pocket book." You will have an easier time getting good grades when you have a direct interest in the content of the paper. Exams, however, are sacred parchments that you will have no influence over regarding their content or form.

Why Worry About Grades?

One view is that your grades in university or college are in inverse proportion to your business and financial success. GPA = "Grade Point Average" where A =4, B = 3, C = 2, D = I and F =0

GPA	PROBABLE CAREER
3.5-4.0	Accountant
2.5-3.5	Banker
1.5-2.5	Lawyer
0-1.5	Millionaire entrepreneur employing accountants, bankers and lawyers.

The idea behind this illustration is that degrees can limit creative thought about what could have been achieved without academic qualifications. In this sense, degrees and formal education can be a "security ceiling" from which there is only a difficult escape. However, successful entrepreneurs (who would often prefer not to perform according to others' standards) are the exception rather than the rule (most businesses fail) - and, there are millionaire academics! There are also scholars who claim that the riches of their knowledge far surpass anything the world has to offer, including money. It seems that success in life is far more complex than becoming either an entrepreneur or a scholar.

Your ability to adjust to a wide range of demands is what the world wants to see that you can do! Someone once said that a degree is a measure of how well you can solve a wide range of small and picky problems, or a measure of your endurance of B.S. (which exists in every environment). While we don't completely agree, there is some reality to it. If you can't put up with the smaller, somewhat complex problems, and manage information at university, how can we expect you to tackle larger and more complex problems when you graduate?

Learn How to Take Tests

After you graduate from a certificate program (usually one year), diploma program (usually two years) or degree program (usually four years), there are often tests you have to pass to gain employment. Government jobs often have tests of mental ability or job knowledge that you must excel at to compete with the other applicants. Various technical areas have their certification exams. For example, lawyers have to pass the bar exam, and accountants have to pass the accountancy exam. We will help you learn about how to deal with such tests in this book. The same skills and techniques apply when taking most tests at college. Knowing how to take various types of tests will give you a competitive advantage. If you want to build a solid foundation for your house, you will have to gear up to become more competitive as a test taker.

Be Self-directed

Take the initiative to plan your schedule and your work. Get to the library early enough to dig through all the ideas to write interesting papers. Study early enough to succeed on exams. Participate in class. Interact with your instructor and ask for help when you need it, and so on. Most adult educators don't want to play "high school" and accept excuses about why you want to turn in an assignment late, especially if they are obvious.

The OBVIOUS WHINER Excuse List

1. The printer cartridge ran out of ink.
2. I had car trouble.
3. I was sick with a terrible headache.
4. My alarm didn't work.
5. I forgot to check my calendar for the assignment's due date.

The list of excuses goes on like this ad nauseum. Instructors have heard these things hundreds of times and aren't impressed that you are serious about learning when you use them. You are expected to get quality work done on time or have very good reasons why you were not able to do so.

Try some of these more believable reasons - but only if you are telling the truth, and only if you call the instructor before the day the assignment is due to ask for an extension (and then only if your instructor allows such graces).

1. I failed to organize my time well enough to allow for the unexpected interruptions I encountered.
2. My aunt died and I had to go to her funeral.
3. My child was seriously ill with pneumonia and I had to take her to the hospital and stay with her overnight.
4. I had to take on extra work this month to make ends meet.

These are examples of legitimate reasons most teachers will accept.

Take Charge of Your Education

There are a group of people at post-secondary institutions of higher learning who are serious about serving the needs of students. You will find them in the Student Services office. They are counsellors, course and program planners, and registration and records officials. They often think of themselves as having primary responsibility for offering consistent, quality service to students. Go to these people if you are having a problem.

Some instructors spend a great deal of personal time with students and also meet needs exceedingly well. You will hear about them from other students. Their classes will be overflowing with waiting lists. However, almost everyone else is trying to accomplish the tasks of their jobs, and most college officials, including instructors, don't have "meet the needs of students" at the top of their job descriptions. Perhaps they should, but they may be under pressure to come up with next year's budget, plan for next semester's course outline, create the exam that they have to give tomorrow, complete research on time so they can get tenure, mark papers so that students don't get frustrated, and so on. Most colleges and universities hire their academic faculty for their academic qualifications, not because of their willingness, ability and track record of teaching well or helping students.

There are other problems you may encounter. You may find that the classes you want don't exist because of budget cuts; faculty wage increases have resulted in fewer sections of courses being offered; the registration office lost your registration file; and, the student loan office cannot find the check you need to pay your registration fees. The "'system" can be a hassle. One student did not get a letter of acceptance into a program. He assumed that he was not accepted and didn't call to find out why he did not receive a written notice. He lost his space in a program he was accepted in because, for some reason, the letter either got lost or the mail failed to deliver it. The moral of this story: don't expect anyone to "molly coddle" you or treat you like you need help, because you probably won't find much sympathy or response. In fact, many faculty members are against helping students in any way - they feel it is "hand holding" with adults "who shouldn't be here if they can't hack it." If you have a problem, you have to take initiative to solve it. Ask for assistance (not "help") but take the primary responsibility for getting results yourself.

Prepare for Success

In some colleges and universities, the dropout rates from the first year exceeds 50%! A growing percentage of colleges and universities have student orientation programs, student success programs and courses, and provide students with assistance through writing centres, library research assistants, and teaching assistants. Unfortunately, these amenities may be considered luxuries during times of shrinking budgets. Therefore, institutions fail to adequately prepare students for what they will face at school, and fail in significant ways to assist them to succeed in their first year. They do not have a philosophy of student success, don't have programs to maximize it, and frequently don't get results in preventing failure. So, the traditional approach is the "sink or swim" approach, which may not work well for the student who may not show up for their sophomore year.

So what does this mean for you? Here are some suggestions you can make sure you don't sink.

1. Read this book faithfully.
2. Go to your student services office and find out what programs and courses are offered for student success.
3. Sign up early for the courses you need, ideally the year before you plan to go to college or university.
4. Spend time enquiring how to get the most from the experts who are in your courses and programs. Talk with them honestly and don't use up a lot of their time. They have often taken training in how to assist students to succeed.

In the end, it is you who must learn and apply the principles and practices of success. Even if you are doing satisfactorily (getting "C's" or "B's"), you can likely learn to do better. Getting better grades can position you for success when it comes time to compete for a job, as more and more employers are looking at grades to judge your hireability.

Establish Credibility with Your Professors

Avoid the common problems listed above and follow the recommendations outlined, and you will be seen as a serious student who is mature enough to realize that you are building your future life, and your future opportunities. You know how competitive the world is becoming. Being seen as a serious student is important because it causes instructors to recommend you as a responsible, success-oriented person when they are called by your prospective employers for a reference. They also will be more likely to assist you, communicate with you, and promote you in other ways if you are seen as the kind of person who will represent the university and the instructor well when you go to work.

Yes, professors and universities care about their reputations. You are going to be a part of your university or college's reputation. You are considered their "product" by some important members of the community. And, if you want to go to most graduate schools after you get a degree, you better make sure that you had "B" grades or better in your undergraduate work (and at least A- grades for law schools), and that your professors will recommend you as a credible and responsible person.

The Tangible and Intangible Benefits of Higher Education

Increased Earning Power

You will significantly increase your income as you increase your education. A high school graduate starting out in the work force at age 18 is likely to earn minimum wage, plus a dollar or two. If the same person attends college for two years and receives a diploma in a technical or service industry, his or her earning potential would be more than two to three times that amount.

A high school graduate typically earns $15,000-$20,000 per year the first year after graduation. (See chart below.) A diploma (two year) college graduate earns from $28,000 to $35,000 to start. A person with a four year degree earns from $32,000 to $41,000 to start. As you can see, it wouldn't take long for the more educated person to catch up to the high school graduate in total earnings for the first 10 years after high school.

Although these figures can vary depending on the type of job, geographic location and other factors, we can use them for comparative purposes in the chart below. Where you see a minus (-) sign, it represents the expenses of going to school full time. A plus (+) sign represents income from working full time. We used the lower income figures above to calculate comparisons. For the purpose of clarity and simplicity, the calculations were made without taking into consideration that most people would get raises and cost of living allowances as their number of years of employment increase. The cost of each year of education, room, board and expenses was calculated at $13,000.

Comparing Expenses and Earnings of Three Levels of Education (after graduation)

Total Income **Level of Education**	**End Year 4**	**End Year 8**	**End Year 12**	**End Year 16**
High School	+$52,000	$104,000	+$156,000	+ 199,000
2 Year Dip.	+$30,000	$4,142,000	$4,310,000	$4,896,000
4 Year Deg.	*($52,000)*	*($76,000)*	4,288,000	41,184,000

Another chart will illustrate to you the effect of education on income:

Median Annual Income, by Level of Education, 1990-2004

	Elementary/secondary			College					
Sex Gender and year	**Less than 9th grade**	**9th to 12th grade, no completion[1]**	**High school completion (includes equivalency)[2]**	**Some college, no degree[3]**	**Associate degree[4]**	**Bachelor's[5]**	**Master's[4]**	**Profes-sional[4]**	**Doc-torate[4]**
Men									
2000	20,789	25,095	34,303	40,337	41,952	56,334	68,322	99,411	80,250
2001	21,361	26,209	34,723	41,045	42,776	55,929	70,899	100,000	86,965
2002	20,919	25,903	33,206	40,851	42,856	56,077	67,281	100,000	83,305
2003	21,217	26,468	35,412	41,348	42,871	56,502	70,640	100,000	87,131
2004	21,659	26,277	35,725	41,895	44,404	57,220	71,530	100,000	82,401
Women									
2000	15,978	17,919	24,970	28,697	31,071	40,415	50,139	58,957	57,081
2001	16,691	19,156	25,303	30,418	32,153	40,994	50,669	61,748	62,123
2002	16,510	19,307	25,182	29,400	31,625	40,853	48,890	57,018	65,715
2003	16,907	18,938	26,074	30,142	32,253	41,327	50,163	66,491	67,214
2004	17,023	19,162	26,029	30,816	33,481	41,681	51,316	75,036	68,875

Source: U.S. Dept. of Commerce, Bureau of the Census, Current Population Reports, Series P-60, "Money Income of Households, Families, and Persons in the United States," "Income, Poverty, and Valuation of Noncash Benefits," various years; and Series P-60, "Money Income in the United States," various years. From *Digest of Education Statistics 2005.*

With more education, you will have many opportunities to stretch and develop your intellectual abilities to their maximum:

- You can learn how to learn more quickly and efficiently.
- You will improve your problem solving and decision making abilities by improving your capacity to handle complex information.

As a result, you will be more capable of dealing with a future of change, be more employable and earn more dollars for every hour you work.

Increased Freedom of Choice for Personal and Career Options

The more education you have (especially if it is attuned to the demands of a constantly changing job market), the more job options and opportunities you will have open to you.

Check employment trends and engage in formal education programs that are less likely to become obsolete. Keep updated in your chosen field. Don't be like, for example, the Swiss watchmaker who was out of a job by 1975. By then, nearly all of the Swiss movement watches were made obsolete because of the quartz crystal timepieces that replaced them.

To state this most simply, more education opens more and bigger doors.

Enhanced Personal and Professional Status

When you receive a diploma or degree, you are believed by most people to be smarter, more dedicated, more professional, and less likely to depend on others for your success. People generally look up to people who are willing to commit themselves to a life of learning, gaining knowledge and pursuing their dreams. The opposite is true for people who get stuck in a job they don't like (one survey noted that more than 80% of people surveyed did not like their current jobs!) So, study and do homework now to get ahead, and avoid being stuck in a dead-end job that drives you crazy or bores you silly..

Increased Likelihood of Health and Longevity

Graduates of colleges and universities live longer, healthier lives on average. Health and longevity may depend upon which career you choose, but your increased freedom of choice will contribute to your enjoyment of lower stress levels, greater job satisfaction and upward mobility.

Enhanced Self-confidence, Self-esteem and Status

As much as some students downplay the importance of a diploma or degree, when they actually get one into their hands, something happens. The fact that graduates have more skills and abilities, they often feel greater confidence and see themselves in a more positive light. They believe that they have passed one of society's tests of being a person who can make a contribution. Society recognizes this fact by paying you more, promoting you more often and by putting you into positions of increasing complexity and responsibility. There is something to be said for learning how to think clearly, to solve problems better, to write professionally, and to present yourself verbally in more professional ways.

Improved Satisfaction with Your Achievement in Life

By getting a college or university education you, can avoid the career ruts and lifestyle merry-go-rounds that so many people get stuck in. You can position yourself to realize your goals and then your dreams. You can have a sense of satisfaction that you have achieved what you set out to achieve. You will respect yourself more as a person who you can trust to do what you plan to do!

Greater Flexibility in Designing Your Lifestyle

Once you get settled into your chosen field of work, you will have greater financial power and more options open to you to create the kind of lifestyle you really want. As your education level increases, you are more able to select the kind of a job that fits your future plan of where you want to live, what you want to do and what hours you want to work.

Make Your Parents and Others Happy by Being Successful

If you aren't a parent, you can't imagine how good it feels to see your kids succeed to the extent that they will be happy and will not stay home forever and wreck your plans for retirement. More seriously, it is important for all of us to give back something of value to those who care about us and support us through our time of getting ready for life. Succeeding in college or university will give those you love a big boost of pride, satisfaction, and gratification. They invested time, care and money in you and they are getting a return on their investment that is far more valuable than money: happiness.

Insurance against Unemployment

By the year 2000, over 25% of all jobs required at least two years of post-secondary technical training. You can help ensure that you will have a job by taking even your first semester very seriously. It is a valid way to fight your own unemployment. Reference?

Myths about People Who Have Some Post-secondary Education

Some of the myths about education are so far from the truth, you really have to wonder how they have managed to be around so long. Nevertheless, they are still here, fuelled by the power of the unique circumstance, and isolated cases that tend to be generalized to include everyone. Let's consider a few.

Myth #1: They Can't Get the Jobs They Want

This myth has been around for as long as we can remember, but in recent years it seems to have become more widespread. People now seem to be quite frightened by what they perceive to be a shrinking job market. Its probably not surprising, when you consider all of the instability in the world, the speed at which things are changing, and the fact that many jobs are not only going away, they are disappearing forever. Also, it is disturbing because, while people go to college or university for a variety of reasons, their primary reason for enrolling and choosing one course of study or another is to get a good job and one that offers a career. The last thing they want to hear is that their career area is closing shop.

But let's not panic. As FORTUNE magazine made it clear in the mid 90s, very dramatic changes are taking place in the job market. The report made it clear that some of these changes ought to give us reason to be concerned. At the same time, however, the report (citing a US Bureau of Labor Statistic) reminded us that the number of available jobs in America would go up by more than 23 million between 1991 and the year 2005.

People who have more education can apply for a wider range of job opportunities, will be perceived as more qualified, and will eventually get a job if they know how to prepare for and succeed in the all important interview.

Myth #2: They Never Recover From the Cost of Getting an Education

For most people, except perhaps successful entrepreneurs, post-secondary education will have a long-term profound impact on their earning power. Of course it may depend on the field you choose to enter (lawyers often make more than teachers, for example) but, generally, it will take you as many years of working as the years you went to college or university to compensate you for the expense of attending college or university. However, the payback is that the years after that can be considered "gravy."

Myth #3: They Don't Have Experience in the "Real World"

It is true that young college graduates do not have as much work experience as someone who went to work instead of going to college. But an employer looking for a person to handle information, deal with complexity, communicate with others, solve problems and be confident would look for a college graduate.

College prepares you to become capable of doing these things better than an entry-level job does. It forces you to take individual responsibility to think originally, organize your own schedule and life, be accountable to complete difficult assignments on time, and work with other people in teams on class assignments. So, while we look at each person's unique capabilities to determine whether they can do a job, their education level enhances their employability.

Why Go to College or University Now?

We would like to make a case for why you should get an education and get it now - a lecture you might think you don't need! After all, why do YOU need to be convinced about the value of getting an education? We know that if you didn't think that there was some value in going to college or university, you wouldn't even be thinking about showing up, and you certainly wouldn't be reading this.

But we also know that, regardless of what you think now, you are likely to develop some doubts at some point in your first year about the value of pursuing an education. At the very least, you are likely to think of some reasons why it's okay for you to delay your education for a while. Why?

Because there will come a time, more than once, in your first year when you are either not doing as well as you would like to be doing, or your personal life circumstances are making it outrageously uncomfortable for you to do well. Unfortunately, once this happens, the negative headspace sets in.

This negative headspace is bad news because it seems to distort a student's assessment of the value of education. This seems to be especially true for students who haven't already fully thought through the benefits of having an education. These students become tempted to buy into some of the myths about having an education. They also have a tendency to misinterpret some of the realities. The issue for them at that point is not an objective assessment of what value there is in getting an education; rather, it becomes more an exercise in trying to make negative headspace go away.

Costs Will Continually Rise

As time goes by, we will see the costs of post-secondary education increasing. As state and provincial governments go into more debt (or try to bail out of national debt), they will have less money for education and social programs, including student loans. Budgets of many colleges and universities are being cut as you read this. Plans to increase tuition costs, book costs, parking fees and student fees are occurring as you read this. Accessibility to education is becoming more important for every nation to remain globally competitive, but their resources to educate people are shrinking. We hope that it won't happen, but in the future it is possible that only the wealthy will be able to attend post-secondary private institutions. Getting your education now is a safeguard against such unpredictable outcomes.

There May Be Lack of Support for Public Education in the Future Due to an Aging Population

Voters are getting older. To some extent, they decide how much money will be spent on higher education by voting on certain candidates. If the "grey heads" (or bald heads) have to decide between 1) providing higher education to their children or grand children, or 2) a minimum survival retirement and medical plan for themselves, which do you think they will choose? Right.

Elitism and More Difficult Entrance Requirements Will Be on the Increase

As the rich get richer and the poor get poorer in the next decade, those who have more money will fill the spaces in higher education. Government student loan programs have become leaner and will become leaner yet. In order to cope with the demand for space, colleges and universities are raising their standards for admission to the institutions, and even to courses and programs. As standards go up, only those with higher grades in high school and first year of college will be allowed to attend.

Employers Will Require More Difficult Testing Criteria

In the past 10 years, many employers, particularly big business and government, have become expert in defining the exact requirements for success in performing particular jobs. As a result, many of them have developed specialized screening examinations that presumably have been "'validated." If you don't pass these tests, you don't even get an interview - no matter who you are or how competently you could actually do the job. We have seen graduates of our programs who had already been performing well on the job (as temporary employees) be required to take such tests of mental ability and be released from their positions as a result.

Jobs Will Require More Technical Specialization for Entrance and Continuance in Future Jobs

As jobs become more technically specialized in the future, the training will become more specific. What happened in the industrial age will happen in the information age. Some jobs will become obsolete. Retraining will be necessary. Staying up-to-date will be critical. For example, a general degree in criminology may not be adequate. You may need a specialization in electronic surveillance systems to get hired for some jobs in the criminal justice system.

Building a foundation of strong skills (such as learning to learn, writing, problem solving, decision making, researching) by getting a post-secondary education now will enhance your chances of future success in an ever faster-changing world.

Conclusion

We have painted a somewhat bleak picture, because you may have to deal with some of the difficulties outlined above. Some futurists disagree about this pessimistic view and argue that technological, economic and social planning will get us out of and prevent such woes.

There will be, as there always have been, people who will succeed no matter how difficult things become. We want you to be among those people. Then you will be in a position to help those who are struggling more than you are. We suggest that when you see storm clouds gathering on the horizon, that you prepare for rain now, even though the storm clouds may pass to the north or the south of your locale.

Chapter Seven

Is Your Life in Order?

If you don't know where you are going or how to get there, you will probably end up there.
TERRY ANDERSON

Introduction

This chapter focuses on two areas: what you can do to clarify your vision of your future, your purpose, values, goals and plans, and what you can do to prepare your external environments to support you to have a more successful college or university experience. We will attempt to give you a blueprint for the design of a house that will stand in the face of the stiff competition and the storms of 21st century change.

A television newscast once outlined budget cutbacks in post-secondary education in the Northwest. The newscaster mentioned that students with higher grades from last year are allowed to register first, then new students with higher grades from high school, then returning students with lower grades, then new students with lower grades from high school (if there is any room left). In most cases, at each institution there were between 500 and 1000 students who could not get any courses. Many students have to slow down the completion of their education because they can only get into one or two courses (instead of the usual full load of five courses). These conditions make it even more important for you to do well before and after you enter college or university. This chapter will help you get ready on the inside and set up your environment for success.

Begin From the Inside Out to Build Motivation

Clarity of direction and motivation are directly related. Clarity and motivation are two major difficulties that many students face before they enter college, while they attend and after they graduate. These two factors probably account for much of the frustration and failure that many students experience. It is not easy to find clarity of vision for your future but there are some steps you can take to produce a tentative statement of what you want your life and career to be like in five to ten years.

Formulate an Inspiring and Motivating Vision of Your Future

Now we will ask you to go through an exercise to focus what you know about yourself right now. You will be able to distil the knowledge into a well organized vision statement for your future. This exercise will assist you to become more clear about who you are, what you want and why. The added clarity will give you a laser beam focus that will fuel your motivational system. The clearer it is, the surer you are of it, the more it will remind you of your commitment to bringing it into reality. Going through this process, consciously or unconsciously, is what gets people moving forward to realize their dreams. If some things do not become clear to you on your first time completing this exercise, that's fine, clarity comes as time goes by and as you continue to seek for greater clarity.

The process in visual form has building blocks that look like this.

7. Career Plans

6. Educational Plans

5. Goals Specification

4. Values and Ethics Specification

3. Purpose Specification

2. Vision Clarification

1. Beliefs and Identity Clarification

If you leave out one of the building blocks, your building will not have the strength or power it otherwise would. Outlined below are the explanations of what each of the main building blocks are and spaces for you to attempt to state, in your own words, what your inner architecture looks like.

BELIEFS are your assumptions about:

- WHAT is going on here in this universe.
- What is true, real, false, unreal, good and bad.
- What is the origin, source and purpose of life.
- What is at the foundation of your life.
- How life and love should be conducted.

Your beliefs are the foundation of everything you think, judge, plan, hope for and seek to achieve. They are the screen through which you filter your world. They form a basis for moral decisions. Some people have very clearly defined assumptions about what they believe is real and true, and others dismiss the issue as "philosophic fuzzy stuff' that they don't want to deal with right now. In order to gain clarity in this area of your life, you can consider some principles that Terry Anderson has outlined in his book in progress, titled, *Understanding Your Personal Search.* These principles can be shared, and practiced, and act as a psychological preparation for what could be called the crisis of the deeper life. This "crisis" or breakthrough point in one's life, can include the following realizations and principles:

1. I identify myself as a responsible agent capable of making my own choices about what I believe to be true.
2. I examine myself to see if there are trends that are self-defeating, self-deflating or destructive to others, and sincerely seek to overcome these.
3. I do not know enough about what is seen and what is unseen - there is always more for me to learn.
4. Assumptions I have previously held somewhat blindly must be examined in light of conscious scrutiny - I must be able to defend my beliefs to myself and others.
5. Searching for more truth results in more discoveries.
6. Failing to search for more truth results in failure to find, which results in despondency and a sense of futility.

Many people avoid this crisis of the "deeper" life as long as possible, but the call to know more, to seek adventure beyond our current understanding is ever present and often conscious in those special moments just before we go to sleep. Many people report having had such experiences of feeling warm, close to self, often report experiencing something beyond self, and define this experience in various ways. Some people claim not to have had these kinds of uniquely mysterious conscious experiences, or, if they have, they may explain them away as figments of their own imaginations.

Principles in the Search Process

There are some principles which Terry has found to be true in his own search for development and clarity in this most difficult area of beliefs.

1. If I believe that it is possible to know more than I currently know about what is seen and what is beyond the seen world, then I am likely to discover more about it.
2. If I seek to know more of what is not known in conventional ways, I am more likely to find it.
3. If I know that it is possible to be deceived, I will probably not get "sucked in" by something which cannot be validated.

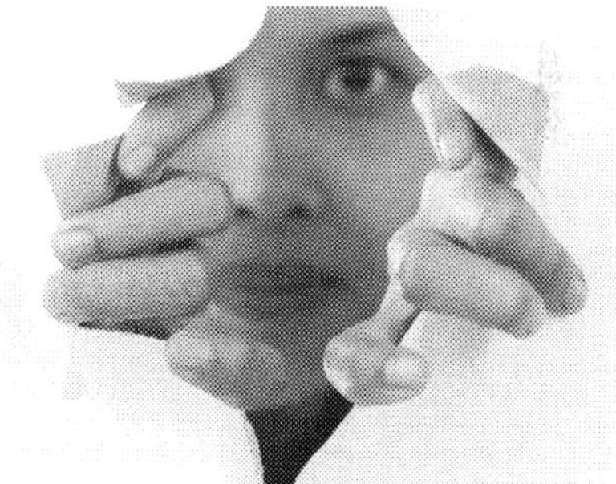

4. If I am willing to accept as true only that which can be validated by multiple ways of knowing, then I am less likely to be deceived by false assumptions. A false assumption may be one which can only be validated by one or only a few criteria. History, science, logic, intuition, archeological evidence and revelation are the ways of knowing that what some people claim has some validity. At least, none of these ways of knowing should invalidate my beliefs.

Increasing clarity will come as you work toward it. Start by giving your best shot at the difficult task of listing the five main beliefs and assumptions that form the foundation of everything you do (such as, "people are ultimately worthwhile," "life is absurd," or "life is ordered by an unseen power," etc.).

Your IDENTITY is based on:

- WHO and WHAT you *believe* you are.
- Experiences with family.
- Experiences with social groups and school.

- Success, failure, and traumatic experiences.
- A vision of what could be possible for you.
- An internal image of what you think others see you as.

Your identity is shaped and limited by the boundaries of your beliefs. You can only consider yourself in relationship to what you assume to be true about the nature of people and the nature of life itself. For example, if you assume, as the existential philosophers do, that life is absurd and has no meaning, then you will consider that you are nothing but a speck of sand on the shore of a shifting universe that may be washed away at any moment. The consequences of such a belief system are that people adopt a philosophy of, "Carpe Diem" (seize the day!) – or translated, "Party now dude, for tomorrow we may die!"

If, on the other hand, you assume that you are a created soul of an intentional Being who knows and cares for you and all people, your view of your identity will be that you and all people are extremely precious - the most valuable of all life forms and more valuable than the most expensive Crown Jewel. Would you trade one of your loved ones for such a gemstone? This is just an example of how our beliefs shape what we can conceive ourselves and others to be. This concept also shapes our belief about our self worth, which is directly lined to what we believe we deserve and what we are willing to do to have it.

List words or phrases that describe who and what you believe you are (such as "visionary leader," "protector of the people," "cool dude," "great musician," "serious scholar," "child of God," etc.)

VISION is a mental picture of what you believe to be possible:

- WHEN dreams are realized.
- For an ennobling future.
- For a preferred future.
- To inspire and motivate self and others.
- Regarding dreams that could come true.

We can only envision what we can conceive of to be possible because of our beliefs and our identity. If we believe we are "stupid" because of previous school experiences, we won't envision ourselves receiving a Ph.D. ten years down the road. If we envision ourselves as having a Ph.D. ten years hence, it is possible that it will occur! So vision is at the beginning of everything we do, whether we are conscious of it or not. Consciously, held visions take on power and energy that may otherwise lie dormant.

For example, one of us had a conversation with a student who cried because he was abused by his father as a child. He felt so worthless. But out of this sad experience emerged a vision of safe children, and a further vision to prevent child abuse for other children. He has started a significant movement in the child abuse field and is responsible for designing and marketing a successful educational program for children. He is making an incredibly good living realizing his vision, and loves what he does.

List the dreams or vision of your future that fit your beliefs and that are most clear in your mind (where and how you will work, live, who you will be with, what you will achieve, etc.).

Purpose (Mission)

> **There is really no insurmountable barrier save your own inherent weakness of purpose.** RALPH WALDO EMERSON

- Purpose of WHY you intend to accomplish your vision.
- Of what you intend to accomplish.
- That sets you on fire.
- That can be life long.
- That emerges from a deep and clear sense of vision.

Having a clear sense of purpose is to understand the reason that underlies what you want to do with your life and career. Purpose "cuts to the chase," "goes for the jugular vein" of our lives and helps us to get in touch with what truly moves us in our hearts and guts. Many

people do not search for and find a sense of clear purpose. As a result, their lives are hollow and they feel that they are stuck on treadmills over which they have no control. Remember what we stated in earlier chapters: In one survey, over 80% of workers reported not finding satisfaction in their work.

Life does not have to be that way. It is possible to gain a clearer sense of purpose by continuing to consciously seek for greater clarity, the same way as outlined in the preceding "beliefs" section. At first, it is difficult to get in touch with this level within ourselves, but it is very important to build your motivation level.

- The greater the clarity of purpose, the more intense the "laser beam" motivation.
- The greater your motivation, the easier it is to concentrate.
- The easier it is to concentrate, the greater your academic success.

As an example of a purpose statement, one student, who wants to become a police administrator, wrote this in her final paper.

> *"I want to protect people from criminal acts because I have an inwardly strong and clear sense that this is the best thing I can do with my life -people, especially vulnerable people - need protection. This fact catches my heart and my attention more than anything else. I will be a preventer of thefts, destruction by drugs and murder."*

Write a statement below that describes why you think it is important to move toward your vision:

VALUES are personal priorities about what's important to you:

- That determine how you go about doing things.
- That determine how you treat people.

- That determine your real priorities.
- That determine how you spend your time.

Once we have a clearer sense of beliefs, vision and purpose, it is easier to sort through all the possible values priorities we could be seduced by in life, and begin to limit ourselves to a focus on the ones that are most important to us. This process of narrowing down our options is called values clarification or specification.

Most people do not really think about much of this stuff seriously. As a result, they set goals, get jobs, and wonder why five years later they are caught in a job they hate. Now they have kids, a mortgage and a car payment and find it difficult to find time to seriously search for the deeper meanings of their lives, let alone go back to school. This pattern is scary and far too common. The values they had when they laid the foundation of their adult lives were to have fun, make some money, buy a car, save money for a house, get married, and have kids. But many people don't do these kinds of things for a higher purpose or for deeper meaning. The unexamined life often feels like it may not be worth living, for some people. For those who want to dig deeper into this area of values, the Values Preference Indicator, a self-assessment instrument that assists you to discover your top 7, middle 7 and lower 7 values priorities and how they really do shape your life, would be very helpful. See the back of this Chapter for ordering information.

List, in order of importance, the nearest and dearest five values that you live by (words that describe values are words like harmony, success, money, peace, spirituality, family, friends or freedom). Check your answers to see that how you use your time actually matches what you say your top five values are. If there is a discrepancy, you may want to consider that you actually have different values or that you should begin to use your time differently, in a way that reflects your values.

ETHICS are formal codes of conduct:

- That are based on values.
- That are agreed upon between parties.
- That are shared by an association of people.
- That can be broken.
- That can have penalties imposed.

Ethics are ways of acting that conform to the agreements of a certain group or association of people. Psychologists, doctors, lawyers, accountants all have professional codes of conduct or ethics that they must follow if they want to continue to practice. If they breach the ethical oaths that they swear to, they can be prevented from working for a period of time, and sometimes for good. In the same way, colleges and universities impose codes of conduct that must be followed, or students can be suspended or expelled for a period of time or even permanently. Dishonesty and manipulative gain are two examples of poor ethics.

An example of a student code of ethics is:

I do my own original thinking and writing, avoid copying others (plagiarism), avoid cheating on exams and take credit for the good work I do myself.

List below the ethics you subscribe to as a student

GOALS that lead to success are:

- Set after beliefs, vision, purpose and values are specified.
- Well defined targets for accomplishment.
- Bound by time lines.
- Worthwhile achieving.

- Realistic and achievable.
- Committed to wholeheartedly.

Goals help bring substance to your dreams and values. When you write a specific goal statement, it is far more likely to be accomplished than if you just think about it. If you post your goals in a place where you see them regularly, check your progress and reward yourself for achievement, your list of accomplishments will increase. A written goal becomes a commitment to get results by a specific date.

List the goals you have for this year that will help you realize your vision and mission (goals like, "I will achieve a 3.2 grade point average," "I will keep my relationship positive with my friends even while I am in school,") etc.

Academic goals ______________________________

Personal Development Goals ______________________________

Social Development ______________________________

Job Goals (During School) ______________________________

Financial Goals ______________________________

Clarifying Your Career Direction

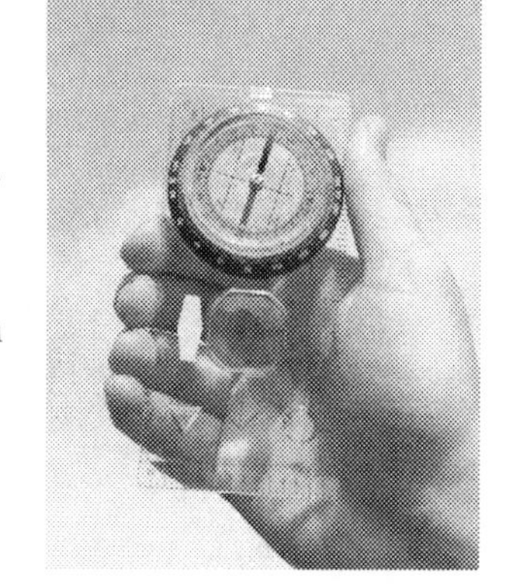

As you become clearer about the above issues, you will find that your thinking about career options will come more into focus. With a more refined sense of vision, purpose, values and goals, it will be easier to sort through the hundreds of career options that you could consider, and probably be successful at. The process involved in clarifying your career direction has three main steps.

1. Expand and explore a wide range of career options.
    - Complete the Campbell Interest Inventory or the Jackson Vocational Interest Inventory at your university counseling centre or on line (http://www.pearsonassessments.com/tests/ciss.htm) and receive assistance in exploring these inventory results.
2. Continue to develop and use your beliefs, vision, mission, purpose and values statements to narrow down the field.

3. Explore the few career titles (that have not been eliminated) in more depth by doing the following:

    - Interview (on the phone or in person) people who perform the jobs you are interested in. Ask them about the downside and upside of the job. Even strangers will often talk with you if you tell them you are in a career search process. They can give you some reality that books and counselors cannot.

List below your five favorite (career) job titles that fit all of the above sections.

Understanding Yourself in the Context of Your Success Environment

A study conducted by the College Entrance Examination Board indicates that students who do well in college or university also do well in other activities. They do well in extra-curricular activities and in academic courses because of two things: Such students have the ability to organize tasks effectively and their ability to organize time effectively. If you want to become a "mean, lean information machine" you will be strengthened by getting organized, avoid wasting time, and do what really counts as first priority.

Let us describe the study environments that are typical of some students who struggle to make it through high school and college. One student spent time trying to study with his stereo on 3/4 volume, lying or sitting on his bed in his bedroom (because desks are for "nerds"), and usually had friends come over to "study." The problem with these particular friends was that they, too, were barely making it through school. This fellow's room was strewn with clean and dirty clothes (unsorted), and sports equipment (from skiing, tennis, bicycling, golf, and hockey). There were lots of magazines lying around that quietly spoke, "look at me, look at me," and the TV in the corner of the room went on spontaneously by itself every 14 minutes. You know what the results were.

Understanding yourself as a person who tends to organize or not organize your environment for success is a very important step toward insuring that you will reach your goals. If you are harmony- or expressive-oriented (see Chapter 4), you tend not to organize the details of your life, which can mean down-time and inefficiency. If you are inefficient, your grades and your social life suffer. If you are the kind of person who doesn't naturally organize your learning environment, then you may find some of the following success action strategies to be worth implementing.

For example, build your best place for study, maximize the environment for comfort, use high tech tools of the trade, and minimize distractions. Below you will get some ideas that you may want to use to protect yourself from being undermined in your efforts to do well and give yourself an advantage from the start of your college career. Remember, how well you do this job will act as a reference for you when you apply for your first career related job after graduation.

Maximize the Environment for Comfort and Minimize Stress

Invest in a comfortable chair you can sit in, at a desk that is comfortable for reading, with a pull out drawer for the keyboard of your computer. Investing in this type of furniture is an important preparation to ensure that, while you are spending hundreds or thousands of hours of your life focusing, you will be comfortable and avoid undue stress. Most students minimize the importance of this, and suffer eyestrain-related headaches, neck aches and backaches on a regular basis, and they think the pain they experience is caused by studying!

Have your eyes tested. Many people have eyesight abnormalities and do not realize it. This is especially true for close work particularly if you are not accustomed to it. You may need to use glasses for extended periods of reading.

The lighting where you study should be bright enough to see well, but not so bright that it causes you to wince while looking onto a glossy textbook page. The light should be behind you so that you can't see into it directly. If you are right handed, put the light behind you over your left shoulder, or over your right shoulder if you are left handed. This way, your hand doesn't get in the way of the light on the page if you are underlining, highlighting text, or making notes.

Build your study environment with study partners who are committed to success, not just friends. Usually friends are not good study partners. You already have too many fun things to do with friends and if they are not fully committed to success, they will drag you down with them. It is better to find study partners who are feeling the pressure of getting on with good grades like you are, than to try to combine study with fun. It usually doesn't work. You end up messing around, going to get something to eat, going to the movies or perhaps even some infamous bar to alleviate the stresses of student life.

Maximize Efficiency with High Technology

A computer is a critical tool to get most jobs done well. The Internet now is the central repository for learning, information, and entertainment. It is also heavily used in university. If you don't have a computer, we suggest that you do your utmost to get one. If finances are a problem, as they are with many students, buy a used computer, either from a shop or through the local paper. It can be as little as a few hundred dollars. Take along someone who knows about computers, if you go to buy one that is used, and investigate the software that comes with it.

Nowadays, new and very thin portables are coming out for under a thousand dollars that will handle most any word processing, database or spreadsheet job you may have as a student for years to come. If finances are tight, here is a suggestion. If you are buying a car in the next year (as many students do during or shortly after high school), get one that costs one thousand dollars less and get a computer with that thousand dollars. It will make a significant difference in how well you are able to do your written assignments. And since written assignments often make up 30%-50% of your final grade, it is smart to place this as a top priority item. A computer will save you time (that you could spend earning money or having fun). Many units have built in word processing, data base and spread sheet programs. Try to get a word processor that has a learning program, spell checker, a grammar checker, thesaurus and outlining program built in - the latest versions of both Microsoft Word for Windows and WordPerfect for Windows have all these features. These features are not luxuries, they are tools that improve your work and save you precious time.

Better yet, most laptops now come with a wireless network card. For less than a hundred dollars, you can get a wireless router that will enable you to sit in that comfy study chair and work away. Alternatively, take it to that nice lawn in your home or nearby quiet park. It may not seem important, but variety in your study environment will help you concentrate better.

Minimize Distractions

The telephone is a major interruption to effective study. Invest in an inexpensive telephone answering system if you have your own telephone line and turn it on during the blocks of time that you have reserved for uninterrupted study. Invest in a telephone that allows you to turn off the ringer, or have others take messages for you when you are studying alone or with key success partners.

Organize your desk and keep it organized. We're not suggesting that you create a sterile work environment, but organize it so you can find things when you want them.

Arrange Financing to Avoid Undue Pressure While You Succeed

Many colleges and universities have scholarships, bursaries and loan programs that some students never even apply for. Talk with the student loans and scholarships officer at the college or university you plan to attend, if possible, one year before you go there. If you have better than a "B" average or have other qualifications that fit various scholarship programs, you may be eligible for free money! One student at our University just received $2500 from a scholarship no one else even applied for!

Government loan programs are well worth investigating and using. In this program, you get to use the public's money interest free until six months after you graduate. Then you often have a decade to pay off the loan at a low interest rate. If you don't have enough money to go to college or university, going into debt to increase your lifetime earning potential can be supported by doing the arithmetic.

You can also begin saving for college years before you go so that you can have the dollars to support you when you get ready to go full- or part-time.

Chapter Eight

Understand the System: Play the Game and Learn

Success is not the key to happiness.
Happiness is the key to success.
If you love what you are doing, you will be successful.

Albert Schweitzer

Introduction

Some students aren't really serious about learning, but they have managed to learn how to "play the game" well enough to succeed. They do their reading, hand assignments in on time, study for tests and get decent grades. However, they go through the motions though the process is meaningless to them, and often so are their assignments. They feel as though they are "plodding" through a seemingly endless list of requirements that others impose upon them, which they simply must conform to and complete to get through. There are a number of occasions, perhaps, that this far-too-typical attitude is justified, but it is possible to diminish their frequency.

It is important to minimize the number of these meaningless events, because going through college or university like this is truly boring and empty. Many students compensate for this lack of meaning and purpose in their lives or studies by becoming party animals, part- or full-time alcoholics, or lost in various other addictions to drugs, fleeting and frequent sexual encounters, food, or a host of cheap thrills that could otherwise have been fun. Such overindulgence frequently leads to misery the next day, further eroding the student's sense of purpose.

If you understand the realities of academic life and the requirements for success, it is more likely that you will succeed. In previous chapters, we focused on the knowledge, skills, tools and style behaviors required to do the job successfully. In the last chapter, we focused on what you can do to get yourself and your environment ready to maximize your success and prevent failure. In this chapter, we will be focusing on realities that you can be aware of while being a student, and that can be your breakthrough for academic success and for learning.

The Academic Challenge: Is it a Sport?

Why think of the challenge of college or university as a sport? We think there are a number of parallels between academic life and sports. These parallels are as follows:

- **Sports are often competitive. So is academic life.** You are constantly competing against standards, and in some classes, against other students (depending on how the instructor grades). Sports have rules. If you don't follow the rules, there will often be penalties. You have to understand what the assignments are, complete them to a high level of quality, study far enough in advance to internalize knowledge for retrieval on exams, and score above a passing grade. If you plagiarize or cheat, you can be penalized or expelled from school.

- **Sports have timelines. You have only a certain time that you can play the game.** The academic game has deadlines for assignments that must be followed or you may be penalized for turning them in late - if you are allowed to do so at all. Tests are only given at specific times and you often cannot take them at any other time (to prevent students who have taken the exam from informing students who will take it later).

- **Sports have practice sessions. So does the game of academe.** Most of your study sessions, whether alone or in groups, can be considered practice sessions - practice (rough drafts) for turning in papers and projects, practice to get ready for exams, and practice to get ready to make oral presentations.

- **Success in sports requires many repetitions. Success in academe does too.** Many beginning university or college students underestimate the amount of practice time it takes to get good at being a student! It can take seven or more repetitions of one piece of separate information in order to achieve an 85% or better recall on an exam. It takes at least that in sports, and usually more, to master a move, a backhand swing, a golf swing, etc. Athletes often engage in thousands of repetitions in order to become adept at a particular skill. It this sense, academic skill is often not as difficult to master as an athletic skill.

- **In sports, the game keeps changing with each new opponent. This is true for school.** Each new opponent, new paper, new exam, new instructor, changes how you must play the game to some extent. Even though you know the basic moves, how you vary the game each time will have an impact on your success rate.

Understanding What it Takes to Win

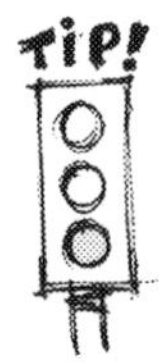

Positive Mental Attitude: The Inner Skill of the Winner

In his studies of professional athletes, Dennis Waitley found that there were specifically identifiable patterns of thought and action that distinguished winners from losers. Other than the obvious things such as desire and practice, the major differences were found in mental attitude, and other, less significant differences, were found in physical ability. He studied winners from many types of sports and found similar success patterns.

One internal ability of winners is the ability to face an apparent problem and see it as a positive challenge. They inwardly control their reactions to an event and assign it the importance that is appropriate to the situation, rather than assess the situation by the intensity or depth of their emotions at the moment.

Winners take "failure" and use it to improve their next performance. Their rationale is, the more times I fail, the more practice I get, the better I get. Because they practice more often without presuming failure to achieve a particular goal, they succeed more often.

People who see themselves as failures often bring low self worth, a history of failure and a desire to achieve their goals through some other means than hard work. Juvenile delinquents, who often do not do well in school, have adopted shortcut methods to getting money through break and enter theft, drug selling, and so on. Students with negative mental attitudes try to take similar approaches when they deal with the stress of studying. They cram at the last minute, fail to give themselves enough time to prepare for exams, write papers in a rush, and sometimes resort to such measures as cheating and pilfering exam items from other students or from the instructor.

In one class, two students conspired together to pull a fire alarm. While everyone was out of the class, they entered the room and picked up a copy from the instructor's desk of the exam they were scheduled to take the following Monday. They had the whole weekend to study the exact study items on the test. They got "A's".

Although we haven't done a study on it, there appear to be several levels of functioning for various groups of people in our society. When you look at the various attitudes and practices of the levels of society below, which level do you see yourself belonging in?

Success Oriented: Top 10%

- Optimistic About Future
- Positive Mental Attitude
- Clear about Beliefs, Vision & Purpose
- Goal Directed and Achievers
- Free of Addictions

Making It: 20%

- Hopeful About Future
- Positive but Reserved Attitude
- Exploring Beliefs, Vision & Purpose

- Goals are Conscious and Partly Reached
- Borderline Addictions

Moving Up Slowly: 35%

- Unsure About Future
- Reserved Mental Attitude
- Aware of a Need for Beliefs, Vision & Purpose
- Actively Seeking Goal Clarity
- Addicted but Overcoming

Barely Making It: 20%

- Pessimistic About Future
- Negative Mental Attitude
- Vague About a Need for Beliefs, Vision & Purpose
- Goals are Tentative and Somewhat Unclear
- Addiction are Established but Unwanted

Not Making It: 15%

- Cynical About Future
- Jaded Mental Attitude
- Mocks Beliefs, Vision & Purpose
- Goals are Destructive
- Lifestyle of Addictions

What "group" do you *want* to be in?

It's More Than a Game: Bring Your Self Into It

Studying can be much more than a game when you are consciously aware that much of what you study can be relevant to your beliefs, vision, purpose, values and goals. To fuel the flame of your motivation, take the responsibility to make each assignment, paper, study session or exam somehow relevant. Few instructors will do this for you. Yes, there will be some meaningless assignments at college, but you can do much to prevent this and make your work interesting. When you do, you will be taking responsibility for your attitude and taking action to ensure that you improve your chances of staying motivated. If you let negative circumstances get in the way of a positive attitude, your motivation will drop significantly.

Stop Whining and Take Back Your Mind

If you tend to be a "whiner," when it comes to getting on with work, consider taking your self by the "scruff of the neck" to command your own life. Otherwise, self-defeating behaviours will dominate your life and work, and you won't achieve your goals. You will kick yourself for years because, when you had the opportunity to move ahead, you blew it because you wanted to just "cruise" or party.

There is a story about a an upper middle class accountant in England (where people are more "class" conscious than in North America) who took his young teen son into the "lower class" area of London. There the son saw, for the first time in his life, hundreds of the depressed jobless, drunks, addicts and hookers on the street, and the squalor that they lived in. His father said to him: "It's up to you whether you want to live like these people or not. No one else can decide for you and no one else can do anything about it for you." Perhaps we all have a lazy part of ourselves that would rather avoid responsibility and seek comfort in some level of "rutdom." Perhaps, if we haven't yet been there, we should all take a drive through that part of town that will help us gain more motivating perspective. Perhaps even more depressing is the middle-class, most of whom are working in jobs they don't like, for bosses who don't respect them, and not finding any real satisfaction in the work they do (which is about 2/5's of their waking life!

Picture yourself five, ten, and twenty years down the road. What will you be doing? Where will you live? Who will you love? What will you be driving? How much money will you have kept for your retirement or enjoyment? What will your salary be? What will your life stand for? What will you be committed to? What is your vision of your future?

Managing Self-Talk Some negative attitudes that can be translated into positive motivators are as follows:

Negative attitude	**Positive Action Motivator**
I hate studying	I will enjoy the freedom and extra money a degree will give me.
I hate statistics	This course will get me into research methods, which I like.
I hate this instructor.............................	I can focus on the relevant content of this course and do well.
I can switch to another section of this course............................	I can postpone this course and take it next year.
I can't concentrate	I can concentrate for 15 minutes at a time. I will take short breaks and get back
I'm not interested in the topic	I will negotiate the topic of this required paper with my Professor.
I don't want to be in school	There isn't a better place for me to get ready for a successful life.

> Some people aren't ready for the responsibility of college. When this is the case, they are best to be honest about it and actively plan to go at it at a later date. It's no use to go in half-hearted. No one else can decide for you and no one else can do anything about it for you.

In summary, when you play the academic game, do everything you can do to make your assignments and study sessions ***personally relevant***. Connect everything you study in some way to your academic interests, your career goals and your personal development goals. None of us wants to learn something about a subject in which we see no relevance, so decide to find relevance in what you do as one of the most important tasks you accomplish in your student career.

Don't wait until you start to have academic problems to get ready for success. Begin preparing yourself to succeed in college or university before you graduate from high school, or the year before you plan to attend college, if at all possible. If you have already begun college, you can take these courses or workshops in the evenings or summers. Here is a list of things you can do to prepare for The Game.

Firm Up Your Abilities Before the Game Starts

- **Take a memory course.** There are a number of these available through the continuing education divisions of colleges and universities. You can also take these courses on audio or video tape. They can help you gain strategies and methods for effective memorization. Check your library for such courses.
- **Take a study skills course.** Most colleges and universities have study skills courses that you can take as a part of your first semester. This book may be required reading in some of these types of courses. Some high school students are wise enough to plan ahead and take such a course in the evenings before they enter college.

- **Take a speed reading course.** They are offered in the same way as the above and can assist you to deal with the large volumes of reading that you will be faced with at college or university.

- **Take a time management course.** This can be a great help in getting ready to take more responsibility for managing your time, which is your life.
- **Take computer courses.** There are a number of evening courses you can take to learn various word processing programs that you may use in your work as a student. You can also learn the skills from the learning programs that come with the software programs, or learn from audio or video programs.
- **Take a critical thinking, or creative thinking, workshop or course.** These types of courses will assist you to get ready to use the mind that you have in more thorough and creative ways.

Select a Program and Courses that Fit Your Interests and Style

You will be encouraged to take courses in which you have an interest, and that you are ready and willing to take. Plan ahead to get into the courses you want by discovering what your career and program interests are. Apply early to get into various colleges, universities and programs. Taking these actions will help position you for success. The same is true for students who are already in college. One of the authors of this book changed his major 5 times before he graduated with a double major in English and Psychology. He continued after each semester to re-examine his goals, career options and lifestyle plans. After he had five jobs in the field of his choice, he decided to teach at a university where he could prepare others for leadership roles, do research, writing, and consulting, and have the lifestyle of a university professor. He has done this quite happily for over 30 years.

Maximize the Success of Your First Semester or Quarter

Your first semester or quarter (depending on the scheduling system used) in college or university is perhaps by far the most important one. If you blow it, it is difficult to make up the lower grade point average in semesters to come. This is especially true if you need a higher grade point average to apply to degree program after your 2 year diploma program, or graduate school after your baccalaureate (B.A., B.Sc., B.R.N., etc.) degree. These more advanced programs often have entrance requirements of at least a "B" average in your undergraduate work. Some require a 3.5 (B+) average for admission. Since you don't often know in your first year whether or not you might want to continue with post-graduate work, it is wise to do everything to keep your options open.

Be Sure You Understand Instructions for Assignments

If you aren't sure what is expected for an assignment, ask the instructor. If she or he is not available or communicative on your first try, don't give up. Make an appointment with your instructor. Ask for 10 minutes at a first meeting and have specific questions written down so you are organized, confident and specific in your requests. Then, after 10 minutes, get out of there. Do not whine or complain in any way. Ask questions, get answers and leave. You will be welcome on your next visit! Be honest about your concern or confusion and openly state that you are seeking guidance about how to do a good job on your assignment or exam. Your instructor will be impressed with your humility and commitment.

You can also meet with students who have successfully taken the course previously and ask them the same questions. Ask them if you can see the "A" paper that they wrote in the same class for the same instructor. You will learn a great deal when you read this paper about how the teacher grades, what the expectations are and what kind of feedback you are likely to get when you get your paper back. You will also see what an "A" paper looks like. This will lower your anxiety and increase your motivation level, particularly if you do it during the first two weeks of class when you are less busy, instead of during the last week of class before the paper is due.

Schedule and Finance your Education to Fit your Lifestyle

Decide how you want to live while you are going to school before you enroll full-time and have it take over your life. Some people prefer to live different life styles than others. There are a number of different ways to complete college. Here are a few of the common options:

1. Full time school (five to six courses per term), no work at all.
2. Full time school (five to six courses per term), part time work.
3. Full time school (five to six courses per term), part time work + student loan.
4. Half time school (three courses), part time work + student loan.
5. Part time school (one to two courses per term), full time work.

Depending on the circumstances in your life, one or more of the above options may be best for you at this time.

If you are unsure of your career goals, then it could be wise to work part- or full-time, take a few courses in the evenings, and get a clearer sense that you can succeed at college. During this time, you can gain clarity about your personal and career direction.

If you have been in the workplace for a number of years, but aren't sure of your direction, the same format could be a wise one for you. You don't want to waste time taking courses that you may never use when post secondary education is so expensive and your time is at a premium.

If you have a clear idea about your career goals, then it could be wise to get on with full-time studies as quickly as possible. It could be to your financial advantage to complete college as soon as possible and get on with your career at a higher wage than you presently earn. If you have family members or children and don't want to put your family life out of balance, you might consider slowing down the pace of your education in order to live a saner life.

Cross check the previous chapter and see that the timeline you design below for completing your education fits with your vision, purpose, values, goals and plans. List your first, second and third priority for your education timeline. Also realize that every year you take to complete your degree(s) is a year that you will be losing income at a higher level! But don't let the money drive you into the ground by cramming, rushing and not enjoying your own education.

Schedule Your Classes to Fit Your Lifestyle

Use the questions below as guidelines to assist you to think clearly about planning your schedule for classes.

- Do you study better at night or in the morning?
- Are you more attentive to lectures in the afternoon or evening?
- Do you have a rigid work schedule that you have to fit college courses into? Some people schedule all their classes on two or three days per week and work or study the other two or three days per week.
- How do you want to live?

Decide these issues first, then arrange your college activities around them as much as possible or you could create an unhappy person or family. Namely, you and those you care about!

When you register for your courses, see if you can fit them into the time frames in which you would most like to schedule your classes. This can not only assist you to balance your lifestyle, but to maximize your success in your courses. You may want to consult your family members or roommates to see if they have any requests or suggestions for your scheduling plan.

Design the ideal plan for how you want your days and weeks to be organized by using the time schedule outlined below.

	Mon	Tues	Wed	Thrs	Fri	Sat	Sun
Hours							
7-8 am							
8-9 am							
9-10 am							
10-11 am							
11am - 12pm							
12-1 pm							
1-2 pm							
2-3 pm							
3-4 pm							
4-5 pm							
5-6 pm							
6-7 pm							
7-8 pm							
8-9 pm							
9-10 pm							
10-11 pm							

Plan the Time of Your Life

You have no option. If you haven't yet invested in a time planner (over 80% of first year students have never used one), you must before you start school. You will have so many assignments due at different times that you will need one place to write down when they are due, and track their completion. You will also have classes, meetings, your work schedule, dates with friends and family, etc., all at different times. Your life is no longer as simple as it likely was! And it will become more complex as you go into your first semester.

If you are the average student, the first few weeks of college or university may seem easy, even compared to high school. No one is looking over your shoulder to make you work. No one is checking up on you. Then, the crunch comes just before midterm exams, and papers are often due at that time as well. You realize that piles of papers are due, exams are imminent, and, if you haven't scheduled everything in a paced, organized fashion over the first 6 weeks, you will have to cram like crazy...so life becomes a scramble. Christmas is a time when you get sick and recover from the flu and from your first semester. This is a pattern we have observed in over half of students in their first semester. But it doesn't have to be this way.

Here is a secret formula we have worked out over the years as we were students, and as we watched thousands of students go through college:

GPA=T x A x R x G x E x T x S

GPA = Higher Grade Point Average =

T = Team learning has power

A = Ability must be exercised

R = Review and rehearse for exams

G = "Grunt" work must be done

E = Enthusiasm for vision is key

T = Timeliness is control

S = Scheduling is critical

You will need to find a time planner that you can live with (a type of calendar that has enough detail on it for you to plan carefully). It is perhaps one of the most critical things you can do to maximize your success and manage your future.

Here are the advantages of using and not using a time planning system:

Advantages of Using a System	**Disadvantages of Not Using a Planner**
Yourmind is clear about when to do what you need to do	You forget things and pay late penalties
Youappear to be organized and professional	You are seen as immature
Youhave more free time and things get done!	You put things off and cram at the last moment
You can write your friends into it	You don't have a social life unless you fail class

You will feel in control..........................You will feel out of control and exhausted

Your grades go up ....Your grades go down

Most college and university bookstores have student time planners or calendars that you can use to keep track of tests, assignment due dates, and other important events. Some of these planners are elaborate project planners that take quite a lot of time and energy to maintain.

Others of them are over simplified calendars that have no room to write much detail. Probably, for most people, a one page per day format will work well for you. We suggest that you examine a number of time planners before you buy one and consider your style of dealing with details before you buy.

Also, consider that you have to carry this thing around with you wherever you go. If you get a thick, heavy one, you know what that means. You probably have enough heavy stuff to carry around without getting a time planner that you have to lug around as well. We prefer time systems that can fit into a coat pocket, briefcase or purse. That way, we are likely to have it with us at all times. We use it several times each day. So will you.

An alternative to a paper planner is a cheap PDA (Personal Digital Assistants). These magic devices can track your contact numbers, maintain your daily, weekly, annual activities, remind you of them, and synchronize with your email calendar and desktop. You can search them for upcoming events or due dates, get them to report all your imminent deadlines, and even look up your schedule on-line wherever you go! The most inexpensive ones are less than 100 dollars. The more advanced ones can be a wireless device, a cell phone and almost a small laptop. One of us has "lived" with a PDA for almost 8 years, taking it everywhere for note taking, for time management, and even for doing things that laptops are used for. So, the choice is yours: hard copy or electronic, track your schedule and keep on top of your life! If you are really high-tech, you might want to use a project tracking software for all of your assignments. Microsoft makes two of them for example, Visio and MS Project.

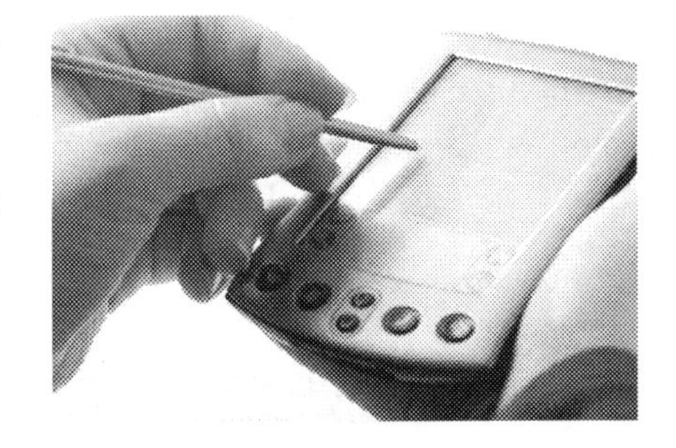

Don't have cash for an electronic PDA? For the "Googleans" among you - and we know there are quite a few out there, - Google Calendar© is free, transportable

around the world wherever there is Internet, and, most of all, has plenty of space to add deadlines, reminders, explanations, and live links to other on-line materials; and, it is fully integrated with other Google tools such as Gmail© and Google Maps©. You can easily get Google Calendar to get a list all upcoming events, appointments, and significant deadlines. At the time of publishing this book, Google Calendar is available in 18 languages, too!

Image Management: Act and Look Serious!

Are you serious about succeeding? Act serious! There is research that indicates that your attendance at class is directly related to your grade point average. "Did I miss anything?" This is a question frequently asked by students after missing a class. Some professors have come up with some creative answers[2]:

Nothing. When we realized you weren't here, we sat with our hands folded on our desk in silence, for the full two hours.

Everything. I gave an exam worth 40% of the grade for this term and assigned some reading due today on which I'm about to handout a quiz worth 50%.

Nothing. None of the content of this course has value or meaning. Take as many days off as you like. Any activities we undertake as a class I assure you will not matter either to you or me and are without purpose.

Everything. A few minutes after we began the last class, a shaft of light descended and an angel or other heavenly being appeared and revealed to us what each woman and man must do to attain divine wisdom in this life and in the hereafter. This is the last time the class will meet before we disperse to bring this good news to all people on earth.

Nothing. When you were not present, nothing significant could have occurred.

Everything. Contained in this classroom is a microcosm of human existence assembled for you to query, examine and ponder. This is not the only place such an opportunity has been gathered, but it was one place...and you were not here.

There is also research to indicate that the closer you sit to the front of class, the more likely you are to hear what is said clearly, interact with the instructor to gain further clarification, and be perceived to be a serious student. You are also less likely to be interacting with other students who, when they sit at the back of class, tend to distract one another, other students, and the instructor. It isn't cool to be seen as one of the high-school-bubble-gummer, baseball-cap-on-backwards crew who tend to go to college because they are bored everywhere, including college. After you get into college, neither instructors nor potential employers are impressed if you continue to look and speak like you are still in high school. You may want to ask your instructor for a job reference next spring if you plan to apply for a summer job. Or, your employer may just decide to call one of your instructors for a reference, even though you didn't list her or him on your resume. Or (this has happened fairly often) your employer who will interview you may be in one of your classes!

When you enter college or university, you are entering a professional environment that has, as a part of its purpose, the desire to create professionals. It is like a club. The university wants its graduates to represent it well in the world and community. Departments, programs, and instructors want to be proud of how you think, write, speak and act. Some of them are presumptuous enough to think that, in part, you are a "product" of their efforts. No one wants to tell you this because it sounds too much like they are trying to do the unspeakable thing of influencing, limiting or even controlling your freedom of choice. But there is some truth in it.

Bizarre appearances, inept speech patterns, a body riddled with punctures or crummy tattoos, or self-centered manners are often tolerated while you are inside the four walls of the college, but as soon as you hit the streets and compete for jobs, you had better know how to act competitively in the ways that you think, write, speak and present yourself. Why not practice while in college? The payoff will entice you to do even more, gradually embracing a pattern of conduct and speech that is positive, responsible, and attractive.

What! I Can't Be Myself?

Of course people shouldn't discriminate against others because of the way they look or speak. But many do. If you want to be more successful, manage the image you project into other people's minds. If you want their respect, find out what they respect, and then reflect those images to them. If you don't care about the consequences of not getting their respect, then do your own "thing" without consideration of the consequences. We don't recommend this latter approach because you can never accurately predict what the consequences will be. It is better to prevent discrimination and help others to not trip over their own biases and preconceptions. In addition, we want you to benefit from our experience. We are not presenting theory. This is really practical stuff rarely spoken of among your peers. Since we have gone through so much effort to write this book about your success, we hope you will heed our advice. Your long-term happiness - academically and professionally - may depend on it.

For example, before going to an interview to get into an academic or career program, or to get a summer job, do some research by making phone calls to people "in the know" who can tell you what to wear, what to say, and what not say. Look, speak, dress, and act like the people who are successful in the field in which you are seeking entrance or employment. Start dressing like the people who do the kind of work you want to do. Observe how they dress at work and casually. And on the weekends wear what you want, and look how you want to look.

Decide if you want the *consequences* of looking like a high school kid who just came from a rock concert dressed in holey Levi's and black leather, a skate board competitor dressed in baggies and long T-shirt (these are typical uniforms of first year students), or a "jock."

> **FACT:** People who look successful and well educated receive preferential treatment in almost all of their social or business encounters...Upper middle class verbal and non-verbal behaviour is rewarded far more often than lower-middle or middle class behaviour.

John T. Molloy, an authority on success and image, has done research on over 60,000 people over a period of more than 26 years. His findings indicate that there is "class" consciousness among people in North America, and that this issue becomes more important as you try to compete for entrance into more sophisticated graduate programs (like law, medicine, education, and professional careers) and jobs or promotions in government and business. Simply put, some decision makers (including some instructors) will judge you (whether they are aware of it or not) and (unfortunately) grade you up or down, include or exclude you, based on how you look, speak and think. Molloy[3] emphasizes the following based on his research.

Molloy asked the following questions of 100 top executives and by far the majority of them answered the same.

1. Does a person have a better chance of a promotion if they know how to dress? **96% said yes.**
2. If there were a course on how to dress and speak successfully, would you send your son or daughter? **100% said yes.**
3. Do you think employee dress affects the general tone of the office? **100% said yes.**
4. Do you think employee dress affects performance? **100% said yes.**
5. Would you hold up a promotion of someone who did not know how to dress properly? **78% said yes.**
6. Would you tell a young person that the way he or she dressed was holding him or her back? **65% said yes.**
7. Do you turn down people who come to an interview dressed improperly? **92% said yes.**

How would you answer these questions if you had decision making power?

Here is a list of "lower-middle class" behaviors that can lose you brownie points in the "upper middle-class" professional world.

Unprofessional Behaviour	**Professional Behaviour**
White socks with dress pants	Socks match color of dress pants
Wearing jeans for dress pants	Wearing 100% wool slacks
Wearing "fashion" clothing to interviews	Wearing quality classic clothing to interviews
Saying, "'N' stuff like that"	Being specific about what you mean
Saying, "uh" to start sentences	Eliminating distracting speech
Having only one style of apparel	Dressing flexibly for the situation
Wearing tennis shoes everywhere	Wearing tennis shoes to play tennis
Speaking from social class	Speaking from educational level
Wearing tattered shoes	Wearing shined, leather shoes
Hair cut with electric clippers	Hair cut with scissors or razor cut
Hair longer (men and women)	Hair shorter (men and women)
Facial hair: beard or long side burns	Moustache only, or none

Cheap watch, expansion bands..............................Thin, gold watch, leather or gold band

Diving or runner's watch for informal ....Wearing same as above

Short sleeved dress shirts ....Long sleeved dress shirts

Make up and hair is flamboyant............................Make up and hair is conservative

Fingernails unkempt or dirty.................................Fingernails trimmed and clean

Cheap pen or pencil ....Quality pen or pencil

These are just some of the signals that build images in people's minds. There are dozens more if you look around. See if you can be more objective in looking at different groups of people to consciously notice what they are communicating about their socio-economic status and goals by their verbal and non-verbal behavior. See if you can objectively notice what you are communicating. Ask others for feedback about the above issues, for starters.

In Conclusion

In learning to play the academic Game, we have pointed out a series of realities that we hope you will examine for yourself and decide how much importance to assign them. Our highest goal in this chapter is that you would learn to play The Game well enough that it would become second nature. Then, the primary focus of your attention can be devoted to learning what is truly important to you, while you take courses at college or university. In doing this, you will be in a better position to manage your future.

In regards to appearance and personal speech issues, we aren't trying to get everyone to look or talk in the same ways, nor are we trying to curb individuality. Neither are we trying to get people to spend their life savings on expensive clothing or accessories. But we are concerned that people do get discriminated against because they do not understand how to create and project an image that the people they seek acceptance from will accept. We want you to be conscious if you are doing things that people will reject you for. At best, we hope that you would become somewhat of a chameleon (a lizard that changes colors in various environments) who does not lose your inner identity.

[1]Waitley. (1979) *The Psychology of Winning.* New York: The Berkeley Publishing Company.

[2]*More Than Our Jobs, an anthology of work writing.* Arsenal Pulp Press, Ltd.: Vancouver, B.C. Canada

[3]Molloy, J.T. (1988) *The New Dress for Success.* Warner Books.

Chapter Nine

Mustering the Motivation to Succeed

MANAGE: To control the direction, operation of. To bring about or contrive. To direct or conduct the affairs or interest of.

CHANGE: To make different; alter; transmute. To become different; vary. To enter upon a new phase. To adopt a new line of argument. To change is to make something other than what it has been. Transmute, transform, transfigure, metamorphose, commute, modify.

There were other reasons why this book came into being. We noticed that the distance between some students and their teachers was widening. We wanted to better understand the true needs of our students as well as the attributes of effective teaching. We wanted to know why some of you drift away from us, from learning, and from your future, while others - in the same class and with the same teacher -

make the eventual leap to take ownership of their learning and long-term career objectives. By writing this book we wanted to first acknowledge the challenges in post-secondary learning, and articulate effective, reliable strategies that have been proven successful. Giving up school is quite simple and easy. The consequences, however, are not. A successful student is more focused, directed, and satisfied. A successful teacher is is not different and paves the student's path to learning and success. It made sense to explore ways to make each group more successful.

Many teachers have an insatiable appetite for learning new ways to approach old problems. Creating an environment conducive to learning in and outside the classroom is a challenge that impacts both students and teachers. It has required countless books, articles, and workshops. Teaching success symposiums in our schools investigate the latest teaching techniques and best practices in academia. Still, outstanding teaching and effective learning remain elusive.

This book tackles learning from a perspective not dissimilar to solving the Rubik's Cube: from multiple angles. The topic must be explored holistically. From motivation to expectations to effective learning techniques, a wealth of knowledge and experience provided input to this work. We talked to colleagues, reviewed the scientific literature available, and even conducted our own extensive research in order to either support or refute some of the commonly-held beliefs about learning and learners.

The Desire for Success

Should you chart a new course or stay steady on the one you have chosen? If you feel disenfranchised by or disconnected from school (or learning in general), if you cannot find the desire to study and feel somewhat ambivalent toward goals, future, and career success, it is hardly going out on a limb to conclude that perhaps it is time to chart a new course. You are not unique. Scores of students in post-secondary schools also coast along the academic tide often uncertain about - or indifferent to - where they may land. Some studies suggest that this uncertainly about the program of choice and one's field of study tends to dramatically increase attrition rates, especially in the junior years in college. To survive the post-secondary life, a clear understanding of one's goals, needs, and aspirations is critical for long-term success.

Should you find reasons to overhaul or alter your current experiences, should you choose to do away with the corrosive doubt that limits your abilities, the decision must a) be embraced voluntarily, b) emanate from your deep-seated needs, and c) be entirely owned by you and no one else. When we set goals that are meaningful and fulfill our needs, we are more likely to succeed in achieving our objectives.

Some significant questions are worth pondering at the start of your learning journey: What drives your desire? What really are your goals, and what do you really need in life? These are not rhetorical questions. Your reflective answers could lead to a better understanding and articulation of what you want and expect in life. The voice inside you is the animating force that, to a great extent, dictates your actions and choices. It is an often-quite, subtle, but accurate messaging system that governs the directions we take at each corner in our lives. The fortunate among us have learned and know how to listen to it regularly. It reveals aspects of our mindset that either pave or limit our success, and it motivates us to take corrective action when we come across turning points in our lives or face obstacles.

Your Motivation is Your Inner Drive for Learning and is Driven by Your Purpose

When it comes to our inner drive for learning, it turns out we humans share much in common and have very similar responses. Motivation is a pivotal word in literally all human endeavours; it can directly shape not only what we do, but can dramatically improve the odds of success no matter the activity. An example may illustrate our point.

If you are motivated, driven, and determined to climb Mount Everest, it is highly - and we mean highly - possible that you will. You will be compelled by your internal drive to make choices, not to mention sacrifices, to reach the Top of the World. You align your life with that end in site. You willingly and gladly organize your affairs accordingly, from funding to training to planning. You will make clear priorities in your daily activities. You do so not because you are forced to or preached to, but because you "need" to personally triumph over a challenge unrivalled anywhere on the planet. You are motivated by this need deep inside.

Indeed, motivation can save your life. If, while climbing the Everest, you took a dive and fell off a cliff with no one in sight able or willing to help you, your need (determination, motivation) to live is your best chance of survival. The story of Lincoln Hall on a fateful descent from the Top of the World in May 2006 exemplifies a man's drive to prevail over unimaginable obstacles as he tried to stay alive to see his family once more. Motivation can and does, undeniably, alter the course of our lives.

While motivation does not guarantee success, it can radically shape it. Our actions, choices, habits, mindset, and partialities in life are almost entirely predicated on what we believe about ourselves. The more teachers understand student motivation, the more effectively we can influence and probe it, appealing to those senses in each of you that long for success.

To be honest, influencing your motivation is one of the key objectives of this book! While the authors did not wish to control your thoughts, we wished to de-mystify learning obstacles by suggesting ideas that can enhance your learning and its outcome. Now that you have read the book, let us build the foundations for the arguments presented in it. It is imperative that we further explore a topic crucial to academic and professional achievements: mindset.

What's Wrong with a Mindset of Mediocrity?

We have faced some persuasive questions in our classes, offices and hallway conversations with our students. "Why sacrifice so much to climb the Everest", some students ask. "Can't willingness to learn be enough?" "Shouldn't passing the courses suffice?" The main question we think we are being asked is, "What is wrong with being a 'C' student?"

These are provocative questions, no doubt. We must confront them, not only philosophically, but also factually. But before we do, we need to set the stage. Please bear with us!

The truth is that post-secondary education is replete with examples of students who are there not because they want to be, but because they think they should. Many of you struggle in your chosen discipline, trying to lift yourselves up for success to little avail. You neither understand the nature of your struggles, nor can you find resources to meet your needs. It is a very difficult place to be in. What is the problem?

Paramount to combating learning obstacles in school is a sincere knowledge of self and how our thoughts shape our reality. There is much evidence supporting the view that our mindset is a strong predicator of the outcome of our lives. This is truly a mystery, baffling the modern anthropologist, behaviourist, and psychologist. Let us offer an example, a rather philosophical one.

Our perspective on life affects our chances of success. If we believe that life presents us with an abundance of resources, the odds are in our favour to somehow manifest them when we need them most. Conversely, if we fundamentally believe that we are alone and deprived of the necessary means to resolve our challenges, often we neither seek them out, nor do they materialize. One could say that our mindset is a self-fulfilling prophecy unravelling the chapters of our life well before we have finished the introduction!

The mind is an inexplicable contraption. When trained properly, it can discover the intricate secrets of the natural world, solve complex scientific problems, and produce unfathomable systems and processes. Only 50 years ago, a football field of computer equipment was required to do a fraction of what a PC can accomplish now, mainly because the human mind has managed to place more than a billion transistors on a small silicon chip slightly lager than your fingernail. When you allow the mind to wing its flight into new heights of discoveries, it can expand its own limits and shine like a brilliant star. Yet the same mind, when misinformed or misguided, can become a trap, one that can limit, for no reason, our ambitions and aspirations. Sports psychology is founded on the principle that what stops many athletes from reaching the top of the scale in their disciplines is only not their bodies; it is their minds. What sets a champion apart from the rest of the pack, they would say, is the ability to turn negative thoughts into positive energy, picturing success, persistence, and disallowing self-defeat.

Similarly in our academic pursuits, your mind and your belief in your abilities dictate the choices you will make. The mind needs to be trained and aligned toward success. We need to alter our beliefs about ourselves so that they can positively affect the outcome of our endeavours. But how?

Those Subliminal Programs!

The mind, like a computer operating system, has programs guiding its activities. As accurately as a PC, the subliminal messages running through our head provide the propelling forces to guide us in one direction or another. Negative thoughts, pessimistic views, and fear can severely limit our ability to reach potentialities latent within us. The net effect of these messages is similar to self-incarceration and confinement to a prison run by faulty operating beliefs. Some of our students' actions loudly speak of what goes on inside the prison. Because they have not evaluated or considered alternative realities, they are trapped in a world where academic and career success and prosperity in life are simply outside their reach.

The key to unblocking a trapped mind is information and practice. The more it is exposed to positive thoughts and experiences, the better it aligns itself with constructive decisions and outcomes. Indeed, this is the foundation of Appreciative Inquiry, a positive change methodology that is taking organizations and the business sector by storm. AI and Positive Psychology have shown that the more you focus on problems, issues, and limitations, the more of them you will have, and the more limiting your resources. Conversely, if you focus on your own greatness and abilities, if you dream about what you really want and strategise toward it, you are far more likely to not only address the very problem, issues, and limitations you started with, but achieve results beyond what you thought was possible. It is for this reason that AI is being effectively used to re-build organizations, by not focussing on what's wrong, but by stressing what is working well and building on it.

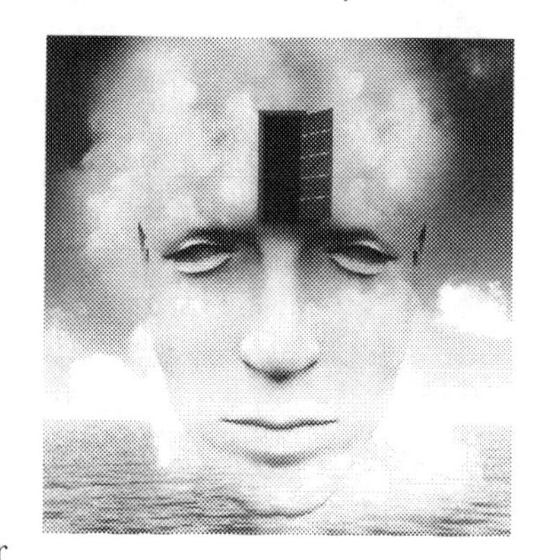

The mind, therefore, is fully capable of reconstructing reality. All we have to do is alter the incoming stimuli. Virtual Reality games, for example, fully exploit that tendency. Take watching an Imax® movie, for example. As that fast-moving plane flies under the Golden Gate Bridge, you duck! That proves that our actions are fundamentally driven by what we perceive to be reality, not reality itself. The mind will assume a liberating course if it is given a chance. Frankly, if you are still reading these pages (and we hope you are!), you are on your way to getting the information you need and making whatever correction your mind needs to be aligned with success. We firmly believe that once the mind examines new realities and adopts a more constructive mindset, a colossal hindrance to learning is lifted; the rest involves planning and effort, and success usually follows.

We digress. Back to the main question, "What is wrong with being a 'C' student?" The answer is NOTHING! Quite often it is as good as a B or even an A, depending on the rest of the arsenal in your bag of competencies. The danger lies in believing that you are only a C student. Behaving accordingly robs you of the riches and bounties we each are entitled to. That defeatist self-concept sets in motion experiences that are rarely satisfying or rewarding. To only go to the Base Camp at the foot of the Everest, especially when you are capable of attempting higher altitudes, leaves you wanting and yearning. You will never taste the splendour of being at or near the top.

The Fun of Mt. Everest

A simple Google© search for Mount Everest reveals a startling fact: Those who attempt and climb Everest often become inspiring leaders and speakers. They travel all over to talk about the joy and satisfaction of making it to the top. If you pay careful attention, you may make an observation about this select group of men and women: They seem liberated, mostly from the prison of self, from the limitations they had previously and unnecessarily imposed on themselves. While they marvel the experience, they will also reflect on the price some pay to meet their objective - life itself. But, they will invariably tell you that the sacrifice and the risks were worth it, because what they got in return was unparalleled with anything else in life: They conquered their minds and gave themselves the gift of confidence. They will tell you how attempting Everest profoundly altered their perceptions of themselves, their realities, and their capabilities

There are probably no Everest conquerors thinking of themselves as a "C" climber. They could not survive the insurmountable challenges along the way. They would give up with the unset of the first crushing storm. They would look up and, fearful of failure, convince themselves to return. In fact, they have every reason to. Their rational faculties, their limbs, longs and muscles all send out the same clear message with each agonizing step: Hard work ahead, it is not safe to proceed. The "C" climber would most likely find a reason, one way or another, to quit.

The "A" climbers, on the other hand, are motivated (because of their need) and already have a vision of being at the top. They know they have physical limitations to overcome; they train for it ceaselessly. They know they can't do it alone; they team up with experienced people to guide them along. They don't have the necessary means financially; they secure the material resources necessary. Even in the midst of the climb itself, they continue to face obstacles of mammoth proportion. Yet, using whatever means available and relying on their drive and determination, the majority of them confidently and ultimately overcome obstacles, not with their bodies, but using their minds. They train themselves psychologically in order to prepare mentally. Using a positive, forward-looking attitude, they believe in abundance; that the mountain will provide all the necessary means for their success. For those who stand at the top of Everest, there is something supremely appealing about trekking their way up from one camp to the next despite the setbacks. Their intestinal fortitude tells them to continue and propels them to make the next step, however difficult and whatever their limitations. Ask Mark Inglis, the first double amputee to reach the summit of Mount Everest on May 16, 2006.

Let's return to your success! How much effort does academic and career success really require, anyway? Clearly, few goals in life demand as much preparation, effort and sacrifice as climbing the Everest. The road to academic success is precious, yet far less costly. It is not the physical sacrifice that poses the most obstacles; it is the mind. Appropriately aligning your beliefs about yourself with forward-looking thoughts, positive objectives and matching behaviours will set you on a course most likely and pleasantly different than the one you are accustomed to.

By no means do we mean to diminish the hard work involved in school. In fact, it can be gruelling; we know. The millennials (that is YOU!) are more after quality, fun and enjoyment in life. This is great. Indeed work and play must go together. Workaholism is no way of living in our view. A successful life needs balance. Yet, we know and see proof among our students that having a purposeful life and being willing to delay gratification a bit can be immeasurably gratifying. As you sacrifice mere "fun" in order to focus on your future, you will find innate abilities within you that will assist you in virtually all circumstances of your life, including having fun! You will gain confidence that you can indeed overcome your mind, even in the moments of relapse and despair, toward objectives that are more than trivial pursuits.

The "C" students will be successful, provided they attempt the courageous climb to B, confident that all the necessary resources they will ever need will be made available if they actually tried. And, once they get to the next camp, it is quite possible, in fact probable, that the great sense of accomplishment will forever change their attitude toward learning. By then, the mind is already accustomed to the rigors of academic life and has tasted the electrifying joy of good results. One never knows! Trekking toward an "A" may then be an option.

A Bit about IQ and Success

We have already discussed Multiple Intelligences. We would like to explore it a bit more to dispell some myths abut intelligence and academic success. Since the inception of Intelligence Quotient (IQ) tests in the early 1900s, a belief began to take shape about mental dexterity and its relationship to one's success. Despite its biases, such as a focus on pure problem solving skills, the IQ and similar tests have been used as the benchmark for defining an individual's intellectual prowess. The academic community, particularly, insisted on the importance of such tests as a measure of one's capacity for learning. Gradually, pure intelligence received increasing attention and was generally accepted as an effective means of accurately assessing student and employee aptitude for success. Numerous studies spawned from the assertion that in order to be successful in life - as a student or professional, - tests similar to the IQ tests could establish an accurate prediction of the outcome.

Well, not so fast, truth be told! While many universities predominantly rely on entrance exams measuring problem solving skills, a new wave has begun to spread over the business and, to some extent, academic communalities. Since the early 1990s, we have not only developed a new understanding of intelligence, we have also redefined and reassessed our measurement of it. The theory of Multiple Intelligences (MI), first proposed by Daniel Goleman, and discussed earlier in this book, has introduced a more holistic view of human intelligence, one that is more inclusive of the capacities and riches all humans are endowed with. Goleman's work has revealed truths about humans being that we probably knew all along. Yet, his work and the subsequent adoption of his theories have provided the context and vocabulary we needed to define intelligence using the framework of human abilities.

There is a gentle revolution underway across various industries. The shift in what constitutes skill is perhaps best appreciated when perusing job advertising Web sites such as Monster.ca. "Excellent communications skills" is often listed close the top of most job requirements. Even applicants to Master and PhD programs at prestigious universities have noticed the shift. Increasingly, the application process assesses the overall qualities of candidates and not merely their logical skills. Letters of reference and detailed, accurate feedback from current and previous coworkers are now replacing aptitude tests in some disciplines.

This gravitation toward a more well-rounded definition of intelligence means a new reality and numerous possibilities for you, the post-secondary graduate. Employers are now looking for those who can intelligently and effectively utilize their natural gifts or learned skills to contribute to organizational life, from communication to problem solving to leadership skills. In fact, at a recent program advisory meeting, we were told by two employers that they no longer emphasize technical skills when hiring new recruits; they have started to focus on interpersonal skills. Their experience has shown that while technical skills can be learnt on the job, emotional intelligence skills are harder to develop, yet are the bigger contributor to organizational success.

This is proof that you can, to an extent, compensate for one type of intelligence by strengthening the others. With increased employment prospects, numerous opportunities are opening up for individuals with a variety of skills. Effectively, the more of these intelligences you possess, the higher the odds of your overall success in life.

By the preceding paragraphs, we do not intend to belittle pure intellectual abilities. Logical problem solving skills are no doubt contributing factors in one's overall success in life. What we mean to say is that they are no longer viewed as the **only** predictor of academic and career potential. There are, and will always be, specialized skills that heavily rely on pure problem solving skills. Success in specialized fields such as mathematics, for example, demands higher IQ scores because they focus on a specialized type of learning. Yet, even brilliant mathematicians often need to collaborate and function in teams, resorting to their multiple intelligences in order to be more effective.

The Big Question

There is a question that plagues the minds of many of our students, regardless of their intellectual abilities. It is rarely asked, yet is loaded with self-doubt and uncertainty. It often resides deep within the student's psyche. And, as usual, its underpinning is the mindset. The question is, "Are great marks or great jobs the privilege of a select few who are naturally gifted?" It is a question probably rooted in fear of failure, one that may be a justification for not trying. In essence, another way of asking this question is: "Do I have the capacity and capability for higher goals in life?"

Our answer, one that is supported by organizations, the business sector, and the academic community, not to mention our own experience as teachers and administrators, is emphatically and unquestionably "YES". Standard measures such as IQ tests are no longer enough to establish your potential for success. One's success in and after school is also dependent on a) motivation to succeed, and b) how you positively and effectively use your natural gifts. The decision to take advantage of our multi-faceted talents and gifts is really ours. We highly recommend a good read of the research we referred to by Debra Vandervoort earlier in this book. It is eye-opening. Really!

Some Hidden Secrets about Teachers and Students

A lot has been written about the new student, or "Generation Y", as some call it. In case you have not noticed, they are all talking about YOU! What many researchers and authors are trying to figure out is where you are coming from and where you are heading. You have enormous influence. Your tendencies, needs, habits, and preferences affect how educational dollars are spent in college education. Consequently, getting to know you better is an imperative in post secondary education.

We teachers form a partnership with you each time our paths cross. We have great interest in that relationship. Like you, we invest quite a bit of time fostering and nurturing it. We talk with you, socialize with you, learn with you, get to know you and even at times quarrel with you! We are with you quite a bit: in our classes, in our offices, when watching you walk across the stage during graduation ceremonies, in our professional conferences, and on multitude of other occasions.

Teachers usually have a profound love for what they do and their subjects. Often we have made a massive investment - personally and financially - to get to where we are. Frequently, we publish books, do research, even facilitate new discoveries, but we rarely give up teaching. It's where we get the buzz! We loath paper work, but do it just so that we can teach. In a way, our professional reality and identity is being a teacher.

From the moment you start a new course, within the first few minutes of meeting a new teacher, you develop an opinion, often accurately, about the kind of learning experience you will have in that course. Some of you seek us out because of our good reputation; others of you dread taking our courses because of our reputation! Well, it works both ways. Teachers also have their preferences in terms of the dynamic and composition of their classes. Since we are all perfect teachers! we often want perfect students, the ones dedicated to learning. But, at times we forget that just like teachers' motivation for outstanding teaching vary, so does a student's motivation to excel in learning.

Naturally, not all teachers have been created equal. Some of us are more conventional and keep a tight leash on the learning activities in our classrooms. Others of us are more relaxed and liberal in our teaching style. While our partnership with you is very meaningful to us, it is not without its tensions. For the faculty, even experienced ones, often the most nervous time of the entire course is walking into the first class and making it through the introductions. We know, just like you do, that first impressions play a big role in how effectively we can impart our knowledge and how interested you will be in what we have to offer. As well, our relationship with you defines our reality as a teacher. If it is strained, we suffer, far more than we let on. If it is thriving, we are in heaven!

We know that you, too, sense some anxiety at the start of a course. You wonder not only about your teacher, but also about each other. You know how important it is to have good chemistry with classmates, since much of the learning in most courses takes place outside the classroom and stems from the interrelationships among peers.

You come to a new course with differing objectives. Some of you want to excel, while others just want to pass. While the desire to succeed as a teacher varies from individual to individual, it is probably safe to say that most of us want to do well in our craft. This derives from an inner yearning to make sense of our world. When we teach you, we are more than presenting techniques and facts; we are presenting part of our objective reality because of our commitment to the subjects we teach. What we teach not only has to make sense to us, but must also be accepted, valued, and embraced by you, our students. If these conditions are not met, our teaching ends up being inconsequential and we may feel as though part of our reality has been rejected. Therefore, excelling in the art of teaching is a cherished desire deep within most teachers. Behind the façade and the external image we project, there is a strong need to connect with you academically and personally.

What are we saying? Teaching is a highly personal profession. Building a connection with you is central to fostering success and creating a climate of learning. It takes two to tango. Without knowing that you are dancing with us, we are there in front of the class all by ourselves, moving around, mumbling a few words, meaninglessly, purposelessly. So, remember the human behind the teacher.

Abundance of Resources for Success

Almost invariably, you have paid to be in school, often in the public post-secondary system. You pay hefty sums to enrol; you give up several years of your youth, and/or give up several years of INCOME, all for one reason: to invest your energies in your future stocks. It makes sense to get the most out of it while you are there. The fact is, while we run our classes and dictate how learning is achieved through our lectures, exercises, exams, evaluation, and final marks, the learning experience is really yours. If your class does not inspire you to learn, there are ways to get your academic needs met.

First and foremost, assume responsibility for your learning, be humble, and admit and welcome the fact that, just like accomplished climbers, you need others to succeed. Most students do. Your first resource is your teacher. Assuming you have a teacher who is caring and dedicated to learning, some constructive, kind feedback will go a long way in changing the learning circumstances for you and everyone in your class. Do not get intimidated. Take chances and approach us. In our experience, students are often apprehensive about reaching out to their instructors. Sometimes one's background and upbringing play a part. For example, in some cultures, asking questions is a sign of disrespect for the teacher; yet in others, it is a sign of weakness. Try to set your inhibitions aside to affect positive change in your classroom. You can!

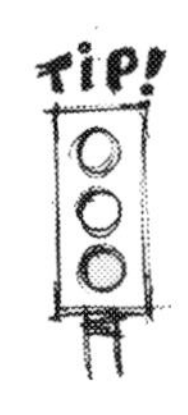

One last comment about teachers and students. Do not get dismayed or disappointed if we are not perfect or make mistakes. Do not take it personally if we seem distracted or distant. Remember, we are humans, too. Just like you, we come in all shades of grey and have varying degrees of interpersonal, academic, and professional skills. But like most humans, we respond favourably to kindness, constructive criticism, and, well, good humour! Keep it light.

The Trap of Victimization

Perhaps two of the deadly sins of learning are indifference and self-victimization. We have encountered scores of students who neither have the courage nor desire to assume responsibility for their learning. If something is not right in their courses, if a teacher is oblivious to their needs, if they do not readily find the resources they need, they resort to blaming others, often the teacher. Unfortunately, many of these students quite often complain about their unsatisfactory learning experience to each other, but rarely to their teacher. By assuming the posture of a victim, they attempt to validate their feelings and beliefs. These students often get swept away by the whirlwind of their own negative rationality. The end result is loss, for the student, and for the teacher. The students give up and the teacher had no clue about their unmet needs. Once again, the mindset ends up dictating the outcome of what could otherwise be a thriving learning experience. Whatever you do, do not be a victim. Most people, including teachers, do not response positively to either blame or self-victimization. Reach out. You may be surprised by the results.

The Next Step

The most insidious obstacles in our learning journey may indeed be our thoughts. Pessimistic subconscious messages governing our minds act as formidable forces that prevent us from realizing the full spectrum of our abilities. Yet, as powerful as our mind can be, it can be altered. As a student, you are blessed with natural gifts and talents. The road to academic and career success begins with a profound desire and need to march to higher grounds. Making the first steps can be life-changing, indeed. It can free you from self-imposed limitations you have assumed about yourself all along. Success in school and beyond is far more accessible to you than you may have imagined.

Let us end this text with two pivotal questions: What do you need in life and how high do you want to trek in your journey to success? If you need to stay where you are, or have decided to retreat to more familiar grounds, you did not need this book. If you have decided otherwise, put this book under your pillow!

Appendix A

The Nature of Outstanding Teaching

To explore strategies for success during and after school, we had to first start with ourselves, the faculty. We needed to form an intimate picture of attributes of outstanding teaching, as they directly impact student success. To substantiate some of the suggestions we have outlined in this book, we needed more than impressions and anecdotal references by our students and colleagues. We needed hard facts and a more concise picture of needs - from the combined perspectives of students and faculty.

To do so, we embarked on a study of outstanding teaching in a post-secondary institution. No such study would be complete if conducted in isolation from the very students who would benefit from its findings. We aimed to discern and formulate the ingredients of successful teaching using views and preferences of our students and faculty members. We chose to zero in on the faculty's side of the educational divide to get to other side, namely, what teacher attributes contribute the most to the success of our students.

We brought together a study[3] group of recognized faculty who had been nominated and won awards for their outstanding teaching. The nomination in this case had been entirely voluntary and initiated by students themselves and not influenced by either faculty or the administration. First, we asked these teachers to delineate what made them so effective. We conducted interviews and focus group meetings to collect over 240 attributes and behaviours of exceptional teachers. With the help of the study group, we refined those attributes down to a 60-question survey, and subsequently sent this survey to hundreds of students and faculty in order to assess the extent to which the views of the study group were supported by other students and faculty, if at all. In all, 640 responded to our survey from both groups (322 students and 318 faculty members). This rate of response statistically guaranteed, with a 95% certainty, that the views of the respondents accurately represented the views of the student body and faculty.

[3] *Samimi, S. 2008. Qualities of Outstanding Teachers That Contribute to Student Success. VDM Verlog Publishing. Saarbrücken, Germany.*

The data analysis resulted in some startling observations. With respect to what effective teaching meant to either side, we found that the students and faculty supported some but not all the competencies outlined in the survey. Chief among the findings of this study was the students' need for practical knowledge. They indicated that when the learning materials are applied and relevant to their long-term career objectives, when they can construct meaning from course contents, they were more motivated and driven to learn. We also found that while this characteristic was near the top ranked competencies among the students, the faculty ranked it much lower in the ranking scale. This, together with a number of other revelations in the responses, made us wonder if there indeed is a continental divide between students and teachers. Let us take one page from that study and present it here as an example.

Top 20 ranked teaching competencies among students

Rank	Competency
1	Welcoming students' questions and being willing to find answers
2	Setting clear evaluation criteria for marked components
3	Testing not only facts, but looking for understanding
4	Structuring the course layer by layer, each with a purpose and clear objectives
5	Being genuinely approachable (words, body language, actions)
6	Mixing practical experience to show relevance of materials
7	Using evaluation to facilitate learning, not to punish
8	Giving extra feedback on students' work
9	Being genuinely passionate about student success
10	Being credible (having experience in the subject matter)
11	Teaching with a high level of energy
12	Demonstrating high standards of conduct
13	Encouraging critical thinking
14	Being connected with the industry in their field of teaching
15	Knowing when students are listening and being able to retain interest
16	Using technology to make learning materials accessible anytime, anywhere

17	Being intellectually curious
18	Appearing emotionally balanced and controlled
19	Creating opportunities for struggling students to improve
20	Using technology with a clear purpose

Top 20 ranked teaching competencies among faculty

Rank	Competency
1	Being able to say "I don't know" without resorting to inaccurate explanations
2	Being genuinely approachable (words, body language, actions)
3	Welcoming students' questions and being willing to find answers
4	Demonstrating high standards of conduct
5	Praising students for their accomplishments
6	Testing not only facts, but looking for understanding
7	Being credible (having experience in the subject matter)
8	Knowing when students are listening and being able to retain interest
9	Teaching with a high level of energy
10	Appearing emotionally balanced and controlled
11	Setting clear evaluation criteria for marked components
12	Being intellectually curious
13	Encouraging critical thinking
14	Using evaluation to facilitate learning, not to punish
15	Being genuinely passionate about student success
16	Modeling a caring attitude in and out of class
17	Keeping one's word on what will be covered and when
18	Creating opportunities for struggling students to improve
19	Treating teaching like performing, being sensitive to the audience
20	Dealing with students as a whole person, regardless of academic standing

By presenting these tables, we wish to demonstrate that, despite our best intentions, we teachers do not always know or understand your needs, or what is pivotal to exceptional teaching. It is feedback, particularly yours, which helps us hone our skills and remain relevant.

We urge you to take the ownership of and assume responsibility for your learning, regardless of whether we are meeting your needs or not. We encourage you to find the resources you need, offer constructive feedback to your teachers, and probe and encourage them to impart and establish the relevance of what they teach. Our relationship is a symbiotic one - the well being of one positively impacts the other. Outstanding teachers need willing and receptive students in order to be able to showcase their skills. Without you, we are reduced to mere presenters. For most teachers, this leads to the demise of both their teaching and professional identify. This is truly a dance that needs practice by both sides.

Times Have Indeed Changed

The adult learner learns differently now than ever before. For example, whereas most of your teachers were not exposed to a PC in their high school years, your affinity for, and comfort with, technology, particularly in the use of computers, are well established and documented. We already know that you have exceptional multi-tasking skills. You can engage in several chat sessions on the Internet, watch TV, listen to music, monitor your cell phone and study, all at the same time! When using a computer, most of you are like fish in water. You are comfortable with it, thrive on it, and indeed learn from it. Some studies have suggested that adult learners get much of their learning from the Internet and using the on-line medium. We see this in our classrooms all the time. When we cannot provide answers to questions, our students can quickly and effortlessly look up answers, often within seconds.

A Word About Your 6th Finger!

You have one. We know! While we applaud your multi-tasking skills and natural affinity for techno gadget of all kinds, your cell phone, your sixth finger as one of our teenagers calls it, can be both a tool and detriment to your success. Use it in wisely. Remember: If you let it out of your hands for few minutes, if you do not look at it 14.5 times an hour, and if you do not keep it under your pillow at nights, life as you know it will not come to a sudden halt, the world will not become instantly dull, and your friends will not desert you. Not only that, by moderating your dependence on your phone, you will find ample free time to tailor your life toward habits that are success-producing.

This is diametrically different than the way most of us boomers studied. This, indeed, is a new reality for us. Our job as teachers is no longer presenting facts, but rather making sense of them. The time has passed to treat the minds of our students as empty vessel meant to be filled with information. Isolating teaching from practical knowledge is a deadly mistake. Students want us to inspire and guide them toward success, help them shed their fears about learning, and direct them on a path to discovery of their own skills and potential. If teaching were only about presenting facts, Google© would be the only teacher we would ever need!

Our study of exceptional teachers substantiated the importance of practical skills as the prerequisites to effective, inspired learning. When we looked at the results, we became certain that a teacher's ability to establish and demonstrate how the learning materials apply to student is pivotal to student motivation for success. As such, practical knowledge is the key to effective teaching and learning. A closer investigation of the two tables above reveals that industry knowledge and credibility (related experience) were in the top 10 competencies among students. Yet, these two attributes do not even appear on the faculty's top ranked lists. Clearly, students' motivation for leaning and succeeding should be at the forefront of our concerns as teachers.

Appendix B

Manage Your Stress to Increase Your Success and Extend Your Future

Chocolate is a perfect food, as wholesome as it is delicious, a beneficent restorer of exhausted power. it is the best friend of those engaged in literary pursuits.
BARON JUSTUS VON LIEBIG, GERMAN CHEMIST

Introduction

This section will introduce you to some of the most important principles and practices of life that you can add to your repertoire of responses. If you can begin management and prevention of stress now, you will be ahead of most of the people you will be competing with. If your physical or psychological health declines because of your failure to manage stress, this loss will overshadow everything else in your life. Your health and the key relationships in your life simply must come first or everything else you may have (such as wealth, fame, position, and so on) will mean little. Here is your chance to introduce yourself to some tested methods for reducing and preventing stress.

Physical, emotional and interpersonal are the main areas where stress can accumulate, and they are all related. When you deal with one, you alleviate the pressure on the others. The person who is overloaded at all levels is the one who is truly stressed. This chapter will assist you to learn strategies you can implement immediately. Start your stress reduction at the level easiest for you. All levels are effective and can have impact on your overall system.

First, let's take a look at the typical stresses you will encounter as a student. Walt Schafer (1992), in the second edition of his book, Stress Management for Wellness, offers us a survey called the *Daily Hassle Index*. By completing this survey, you can better anticipate the types of stress you will encounter and compare your current score with that of other students.

Below is a list of daily hassles that commonly irritate college students. Please indicate how often each one is an irritation to you. Use numbers as follows.

Typical Irritants and Stressors of College Students

Almost never an irritation to me = 0 **Sometimes an irritation to me = 5** **Frequently an irritation to me = 10**		Constant pressures of studying	
		Instructor difficult to understand	
		Not enough close friends	
Parking problems around campus		Not enough time to talk with friends	
Careless bike riders		Too few dates	
Library too noisy		Room temperatures	
Roommate too noisy		How I look	
Preparing meals		Too little intimacy	
Too little time. Too little money		Other students are unfriendly	
Deciding what to wear		Getting to class on time	
Doing laundry		Quality of meals	
Materials unavailable in library		Future plans	
Getting up in the morning		Relationships at work	
My weight		Tensions in love relationship	
Not enough time to exercise		Conflict with family	
Noisy neighbors		Crowds	
Conflicts with roommate		Other drivers	
Instructor not available		Missing my family	
Boring instructor		No mail	

Being lonely		Writing term papers	
Being unorganized		Household chores	
Others' opinions of me		Fixing hair in morning	
Roommate's messiness		Physical safety after dark	
Problems with pets		Car problems	
Too little sleep		**Your Total Score______**	
Shopping		**Average score for males 152;**	
Taking tests		**females 213**	

If you have scores that are higher than average, you might want to talk with a professional such as a university counselor, a doctor or at least a friend about this issue.

The Principles of Stress Management

Your Ideal Stress Load

Each person has an ideal level of stress that he or she can thrive on. If you reduce this ideal, performance and morale go down and if you increase it above the threshold of tolerance, the same negative result will occur. Therefore, it is important to understand your ideal level of stress, recognize the signs of under load or overload, and learn to control your exposure to stress. Otherwise, you may feel like a helpless victim of changes going on around you.

Most students push themselves into overload patterns, rather than under-load. Let's take the example of one student, Eric, age 19, who attends college, and is taking three courses. He works 24 hours per week at a sports store, is a member of a bicycling club that races on Saturdays, wants to spend two or three nights per week with his girlfriend, plans to go fishing or golfing on Sundays with his friend, and wants to have time to watch TV for about 16 hours per week (which he got used to when he was in high school).

Eric makes about $1,200.00 per month at his job, has very little savings from the previous summer, and has to pay $1,200 a year for his car insurance. He was wise enough to save his money during high school to pay cash for his car, but now he has to rebuild the engine at a cost of $1,900.00, and replace the tires at a cost of $600.00.

In addition, after he pays his first semester's tuition, books, and rent in September, he realizes that he will not be able to complete his first semester of college taking three courses and continue his fun lifestyle on his limited income. To add to this pile of stress, his family wants him to spend more time with them; he can't afford fishing tackle, bike repairs, unexpected car repairs, and dollars for recreation so that he can maintain his sanity. He has a very typical dilemma of stress overload that is made more difficult by a lack of cash. He is caught in a catch 22 (or cash 22)! If he doesn't increase his level of education, he will be left behind as more and more jobs in the future require specialized training beyond high school. But unless he sacrifices for a few years now, he won't be able to break through the present ceiling of his earning power to a new earning level. There is no easy way out of his dilemma.

So, like the average student, Eric is forced to live a more impoverished financial lifestyle in order to build a foundation for his future. He feels like he is trapped into living an unacceptable student life style for several years, or postpone college for a few years to "live" for a while. But if he postpones school, he will be falling increasingly behind, losing years of higher earning potential, and limiting his work options. He will have to give up something to get to where he wants to go. The ability to postpone immediate pleasures for longer term ones is the sign of a person destined for increased freedom of choice and success.

Many young people feel as though they are "trapped" into at least two to four years of frustration and feeling "blocked" from pursuing their preferred life style. There are a few students who have a much easier time of it because of parental support, scholarships, and savings plans that were put into place when they were children. But most students experience the stress of this period of time when there is a time and dollar "pinch." And all the stresses outlined above are in addition to the stress experienced by the daily life of being a student, completing assignments, preparing for tests and meeting deadlines.

Yet, in the example above, Eric has it relatively easy! If you are changing careers, a single parent or living in a family as a sole wage earner, your stresses multiply. At first, the amount of stress you face may seem overwhelming, but, with the knowledge and skills outlined in this chapter, you can prepare yourself to deal with the complexity and difficulties you will face as a student. Visualize yourself graduating, having windows of opportunity open to you, eventually getting your preferred job, and reaching your lifestyle goals. You will still have stress in your life. You will need to continue learning to keep up with the rapid changes in your field. But you can learn to learn fast, and reduce your stress.

Stress Can Accumulate and Show up as Symptoms

Unless you have a plan to prevent and manage stress, your stresses will accumulate and show up in the form of symptoms. These symptoms can be the warning signals of more serious and debilitating problems if you don't manage them in advance and prevent their further development. Stress accumulates in the body and emotional system the same way oil gets dirty in a car after a certain number of kilometers. Unless the oil gets changed, additional wear and tear will take its toll on the engine and wear it out early.

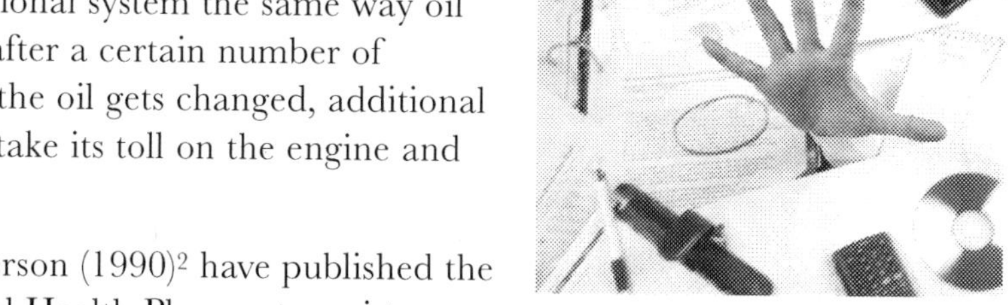

Faulkner and Anderson (1990)[2] have published the Stress Indicator and Health Planner to assist you to diagnose your symptoms of stress in five areas, and plan for increased wellness, performance and enjoyment in life. This planner is comprehensive and can assist you to track levels of stress over time so that you can see progress in your efforts at managing stress.

Typical symptoms of stress could include some of the following.

- Indigestion
- Constipation
- Pain in the neck, shoulders or back
- Fatigue
- Colds or flu
- Headaches
- Allergies
- Feeling worried, guilty, bored, lonely or helpless
- Abuse of alcohol, tobacco or drugs
- Mismanagement of money
- Sleeping or eating more or less than usual.

These are typical of the many symptoms of stress. When you see them cropping up in your life, take action.

Energy Can't Flow Through a Blocked System

You know people who are generally "uptight." They take on more than they can handle, or they try to do too little. They worry about problems instead of taking action. They can't relax and constantly drive themselves, or they attempt very little and are depressed. Their faces show signs of strain and striving or boredom, and they seem to age faster than their contemporaries. They are out of shape physically, often constipated or overweight, often express anger or frustration and rarely claim to be at peace. They may use alcohol, tobacco and drugs to "let go" and divert themselves from their otherwise tense lives. They may have fleeting relationships that don't deepen and they move from one "friend" to the next. They party themselves into a hangover state and then glorify their life style as "free."

This is the profile of many college students, and the negative image sometimes conveyed by fraternity or sorority members - thus the name "frat rat." Fraternities and sororities may promote this type of lifestyle as part of the required pattern of behaviour for acceptance and approval. Under the surface of this profile is often a level of un-dealt-with tension and stress that has accumulated, and an unclear set of goals. These tense people often don't manage their time or their priorities well; they overextend or under extend themselves, do not claim to have clear direction for their lives, are sick more often, and their grades suffer as a result.

Unblocking an Obstructed System

If you see yourself in any of the above typical self-defeating patterns of coping with stress, you can choose to replace these patterns with more healthy ones. You can feel better, extend your delight in life, look healthier and enhance your enjoyment of learning at college or university. We will begin with the assumption that no matter how stress-free your life style has been in the past, you have accumulated a certain amount of stress and have a base line of tension that can be reduced so that your performance and enjoyment can be enhanced.

One quick way to measure your current level of stress is to measure your own SUDS level. SUDS stands for "Subject Units of Distress" and can be measured by your own quick estimate on a 10 point scale:

1= very low stress; and 10 = very high stress level.

We have tried this in our classes on student success at the beginning of the semester - the average level is 3.2 for the students in class. Then we ask them to estimate their level just before the mid-term exam - it goes up to 6.3 for the average student! In fact, here is an account of one of us whose SUDs level escalated: "I was on an airplane returning from a 20th anniversary tour of Europe with my wife. A few minutes ago, without any warning, the fellow behind me quickly ratcheted the back of my reclined seat up because he felt like having more space in front of him."

"Dinner had just been served and he wanted more room. He didn't ask me to move the seat up. My SUDS level moved from 2 to 8. I thought perhaps it was done accidentally so I returned it to its reclining position. He rammed the seat up quicker the second time. I turned around and asked him what he was doing. He said, "I want it up while I eat." The image he conveyed to me was of a "power-tripper," with no consideration or respect for others, no patience to ask - a jerk, pushing his way through life. My first, emotional reaction was to stand up, turn around, and with the lightening speed of my somewhat limited karate training, place my elbow into his eye. My more rational training in the criminal justice system over-rode this first reaction and I began practicing some of my stress management techniques."

Physical Stress Management Methods

These methods involve some type of aerobic exercise and/or breathing techniques. Before beginning some type of regular program, have an overall physical checkup with your doctor to see if there is any reason why you shouldn't push yourself past your usual level of exertion. These methods can involve physical exercise like running, swimming, cycling - anything that increases the use and circulation of oxygen throughout the body. Working up a sweat three or four times a week for twenty or thirty minutes at a time will be helpful in knocking down stress, maximizing energy levels and removing tension blockages from muscles, joints and nerves.

Pushing your heart rate to 70% of its maximum for your age and weight can give you a measurement of the amount of aerobic activity you are engaging in, and guarantees you a workout that gets stress reduction and management results. If you aren't the kind of a person who can commit yourself to such rigorous physical workouts, you can slow it down and stretch it out. Research has found that an hour walk at moderate pace can achieve the same kind of overall results. We find that the more rigorous workouts are more satisfying and produce a relaxing "afterglow." But longer walks can be a time to reflect and get some inspiration, especially if the walks are in the woods or on interesting trails.

Emotional Stress Management Methods

Talk out your stresses with others. This can be a powerful way to bring down stress levels. Research indicates that those who have a network of close friends are more likely to be healthy, miss work less often, live longer and have a higher morale overall. Married people live longer than single people. People who hold things in, rarely talk about their internal concerns, self-doubts, or inadequacies don't gain the benefits of others' points of view about their problems. They are stuck with their own limited solutions!

Open up to others, especially those who are capable of understanding and expanding your perspective of possible solutions. This is a creative way to deal with a wide range of stress-producing problems that may be of an emotional nature, or may be related to finances, relationship stresses, or other areas of life. Seek the assistance of specialists if you are aware of what your special problem area is. Career counselors can help with career counseling, abuse counselors can help with self-worth issues related to having been abused in various ways, and health specialists can assist with stress related issues.

A very useful guide to balancing your brain and enhancing your academic performance is a book by Dr. Daniel Amen.

> [4]*Clinical neuroscientist and psychiatrist Amen uses nuclear brain imaging to diagnose and treat behavioral problems. He explains how the brain works, what happens when things go wrong, and how to optimize brain function. Five sections of the brain are discussed, and case studies clearly illustrate possible problems. The accompanying brain-scan photos are difficult to read with an untrained eye. Although Amen provides step-by-step "prescriptions" geared toward optimizing and healing the different sections of the brain ("create a library of wonderful experiences"; "try meditation/self-hypnosis"), 80 percent of the patients in his case studies were given medication to treat their behavioral problems. The audience for this book is ambiguous. While it encourages readers to evaluate themselves and others, it would be more useful to a professional in the social sciences than to the general reader. (Reviewed by Reed Business Information, Inc.)*

This section is continuously evolving and we authors consider it to be a "work in progress" over the next few months to be enhanced with more input from students and colleagues.

[1]Schafer, W. *Stress Management for Wellness.* Hold, Rinehart and Winston, Inc. Orlando, Florida, 1992.

[2]Faulkner, G. and Anderson, T. *The Stress Indicator and Health Planner.* Consulting Resource Group International, Inc., Abbotsford, B.C. Canada, 1990. 2006.

[3]Amen, Daniel. *Change Your Brain, Change Your Life.* Three Rivers Press, 1999.

[4]Amen, Daniel. *Magnificent Mind at Any Age.* Harmony Books. 2008